Dorothy L. Sayers

Garland Reference Library of the Humanities (Vol. 80)

An Annotated Guide
to the Works of
Dorothy L. Sayers

Robert B. Harmon
and
Margaret A. Burger

Garland Publishing, Inc., New York & London

1977

Library of Congress Cataloging in Publication Data

Harmon, Robert Bartlett, 1932-
    An annotated guide to the works of Dorothy L. Sayers.

    (Garland reference library of the humanities ; 80)
    Includes index.
    1. Sayers, Dorothy Leigh, 1893-1957--Bibliography.
I. Burger, Margaret A., joint author. II. Title.
Z8787 6.55.H37 [PR6037.A95]   016.823'9'12   76-57952
ISBN 0-8240-9896-X

Printed in the United States of America

Contents

PREFACE

The writings of and about Dorothy L. Sayers
present to the bibliographer a formidable set of
problems. Perhaps chief among these is the number
of different media in which she wrote as well as
the different subjects she covered. Many of these
writings appear in more than one form which only
adds to the confusion.

Because of these problems, bibliographic control
becomes exceedingly difficult, if not almost impossible.
As a consequence, what follows can only be termed a
preliminary survey. Numerous persons have assisted
the compilers during their months of work on this
survey. None can properly be charged with any of its
deficiencies, but singly and as a group they must
enjoy a substantial share of the credit for its merits,
since the survey would not have been possible without
them.

We obtained access to essential library resources
through the cooperation of numerous libraries throughout the San Francisco Bay Area. Special thanks are due

Mrs. Margaret Atkins of the San Jose State
University Library for obtaining many needed
materials via inter-library loan. Our appreciation
is also extended to many persons who knew and
associated with Miss Sayers during her lifetime and who have kindly given Miss Burger much
valuable information in their correspondence with
her. Of this group our particular thanks go to
Muriel St. Clare Byrne, O.B.E., for her wealth of
knowledge of Dorothy Sayers which she has so
gracefully shared with us. We would also like to
thank Prof. Clyde Kilby and Miss Barbara Griffin
of the Marion E. Wade Collection at Wheaton College
for allowing us to include their inventory of the
Dorothy L. Sayers Papers in this work.

San Jose and   Robert B. Harmon
Los Gatos, California   Margaret A. Burger
Summer 1976

Dorothy L. Sayers

INTRODUCTION

Most avid readers recognize Dorothy L. Sayers
as an excellent detective fiction writer and the
creator of that most aristocratic of amateur sleuths,
Lord Peter Wimsey. Relatively few, however, are fully
aware that her literary talents encompassed a much
broader spectrum. She was, by temperament and training,
a scholar. She wrote no detective fiction after the
start of the Second World War and spent the majority
of her time thereafter in literary persuits which were
to her far more important and satisfying. She only
undertook detective fiction for the most prosaic of
reasons: "I had to make money somehow." Aside from her
detective fiction she was a scholar of medieval literature,
a poet, translator, Christian apologist, lecturer, playwright, and author of numerous articles covering a wide
variety of subjects.

Dorothy Leigh Sayers was born on June 13, 1893,
in Oxford, England, the daughter of the Reverend Henry
Sayers, sometime headmaster of the Cathedral Choir School,
Oxford, and Helen May (Leigh) Sayers, great niece of

1

Percival Leigh, "the Professor" of Punch, an English
weekly published since 1841 that retains even today its
reputation for satirical humor. It is not improbable
that Dorothy may have inherited from this relative
the dry humor and rapier wit which distinguish both
her religious works and detective novels. Obviously
her religious training occurred within the confines
of the Church of England. Dorothy took her religion
seriously; the struggles between two of its parties,
the Anglo-Catholic and the Evangelistic, later challenged
her to enter the controversy and write her theological
plays and religious essays.

Her youthful years were spent in East Anglia,
known as the fen country, a seventy-mile tract, originally
swampland, where the Romans had first constructed roads
and attempted drainage in England. Undoubtedly she was
greatly influenced by this area, for it is here that
her Peter Wimsey mystery, The Nine Tailors is set.

Dorothy L. Sayers was one of the first women
to obtain an Oxford degree. She attended Somerville
College, which was named after a formidable woman
scholar, and graduated in 1915, attaining first honors
in medieval literature. In Gaudy Night, she made use
of her vivid memories of the College, for Shrewsbury is

Somerville, thinly disguised. Before she was twenty,
she published a small volume of verse, Op. I. This
was followed by Catholic Tales, another collection
of poems which gave an indication of the fine things
to come.

Following her college years, Dorothy Sayers
settled for a time in London where she worked as a
copywriter in a leading advertising agency. It was
here that she learned to write tight, readable prose,
to meet deadlines, to dig up facts, and weigh and present
them accurately. This experience stood her in good
stead when, in 1923, she began to write detective
novels. While she was at Oxford, she made a careful
and critical study of this type of writing.

In her first novel, Whose Body?, Sayers
revitalized the art of the detective story by her
lively prose, her contemporary quality, and by the
invention of a totally new type of detective in Lord
Peter Wimsey. After Clouds of Witness was published
in 1926, a new Lord Peter novel appeared nearly every
year until 1937. Her writings in the detective genre
were interrupted only briefly, in 1929, when she
published Tristan in Brittany, a work of prose and
verse begun while she was at Oxford; but since there

was no market for this type of writing, Sayers
returned to detective fiction the next year. It was
in Strong Poison that she introduced a female
companion for Lord Peter in the person of Harriet
Vane, a scholarly and highly independent young woman
who resembles very much the author herself. The
Wimsey-Vane relationship carried on through three
more novels (including a brief mention of the lady
in Murder Must Advertise) until their marriage on
the stage in 1936 in Busman's Honeymoon.

Dorothy Sayers published her last detective
novel in 1937. She seems to have had some misgivings
about ever having written these kinds of stories
because, as she told one interviewer: "It would be
well to discourage the idea that I am a writer of
mystery-fiction, who in middle age suddenly 'got religion'
and started to preach the gospel...; the truth is the
exact contrary. I was a scholar of my college....
Having, in one way or another, made sufficient money
to live on, I was able to drop the detective fiction,
and go back to the literary criticism, verse translation,
and so on, which I had been trained and qualified to do."

Upon abandoning the detective novel, Miss Sayers
devoted all of her energies to the task which she

regarded as the true purpose of her life--that of
making religion real and vivid for the widest public.
Her second play, The Devil to Pay, was written for
the Canterbury Festival and is a modern version of
the story of Doctor Faustus. This was followed by
a cycle of radio plays for the British Broadcasting
Corporation on the life of Christ, entitled The Man
Born to Be King. It was so successful that it was
produced nearly every year thereafter by the B.B.C.
as its Christmas and Easter attraction.

Miss Sayers also wrote many essays. Her
belief in God as Creator, her philosophy of life,
her judgements on various phases of learning were
expressed in a number of books which include Begin
Here, The Mind of the Maker, and Unpopular Opinions.
Perhaps the most noteworthy efforts were directed
toward a translation of Dante's Divina Commedia.
His natural piety and colloquial idiom had always
attracted her; her own religious life was built on
natural piety and common sense, supported by extensive
reading. Her translations of the Inferno and the
Purgatorio were surely labors of love but were not
overly successful. "She caught the directness of the
original," wrote one critic, "but failed to catch the

poetry. But her prose comments have done more than
those of any other recent English author to quicken
interest in Dante."

During her work on this project, for some
measure of relief, she found time to translate the
earliest and noblest of the French Chansons de Geste,
the Chanson de Roland. After completing this work,
she started to translate Dante's third volume of
the Commedia, Paradiso. This, she found, was most
difficult, perhaps because her energies were flagging
due to failing health. Dorothy L. Sayers died of a
thrombosis on December 17, 1957, having made worthy
contributions to English literature in two very
different fields.

In the 1920's and 1930's, Miss Sayers established
herself as one of the few who could give a new look
to the detective novel. Her recipe was to deftly mix
a plot that kept readers guessing with inside information, told without tears, about some fascinating
subject--campanology, the backrooms of an advertising
agency, and life behind the discreet windows of a West
End club. Lord Peter Wimsey came alive as a good
companion to the few fictional detectives into whom
an engaging personality has been breathed. This was

not accomplished by mere chance; she had made a
close critical study of the craft. Lecturing once
on Aristotle's Poetics, she remarked that he was
obviously hankering after a good detective novel
because he had laid it down that the writer's business
was to lead the reader up to the garden, to make the
murderer's villainy implicit in his character from
the start, and to remember that the denouement is the
most difficult part of the story.

Dorothy L. Sayers was definitely no fly-by-night
writer of thrillers. Not only did she write superbly
constructed detective plots, played out in witty
comedies of manners, she was also a scholar of great
erudition who was to become, after the disappearance
of Lord Peter, one of the outstanding translators
and interpreters of Dante, as well as a formidable
Christian apologist. She has written what is widely
accepted as the best history of the detective story,
and has managed, in addition, to draw the fire of
such notable critics as Edmund Wilson, Q.D. Leavis,
and W.H. Auden, as well as the attention of everyone
who has ever written about detective fiction. Even
though she has been dead for some time, Dorothy L.
Sayers is yet a literary and social phenomenon to be
grappled with.

Section A

NOVELS

Like most works of detective fiction, the novels
of Dorothy L. Sayers have not generally been considered
by most critics as serious works of literature. Sayers
was, however, a sophisticated writer who, conscious
of the major problems involved in writing detective
fiction, insisted that it was and should be considered
as an integral part of the mainstream of literature.
As a corollary, an intimate connection is demonstrated
between Miss Sayers' theory and practice, one stressing
the fact that in her hands the detective novel serves
as a vehicle for a serious exploration of several
thematic concerns that elevate her works above pure
escape literature.

This section is divided into three parts. The
first covers novels written by Miss Sayers herself, and
the second, those written with others or the help of
others. The titles are arranged alphabetically within
each part. Below each title is listed the major editions
in chronological order. Some descriptive comments are

added where appropriate. A third section consists
of collections of two or more novels in one volume.

I. Novels Written by Dorothy L. Sayers

A1. Busman's Honeymoon: a Love Story with Detective

Interruptions.

London: V. Gollancz, 1937.   381p.
New York: Harcourt, Brace, 1937.   381p.
New York: Harper, 1960.   381p.
Harmondsworth ₁Eng.₎ : Penguin Books, 1962.   379p.
London: Gollancz, 1972.   446p. (Collected
  stories, v.14)
London: New English Library, 1974.   397p.

This work was originally thought of, and
produced, as a play (See D1): the subsequent novel
being, in Miss Sayers' words, "but the limbs and
outward flourishes" of the dramatic work. In
writing this story Miss Sayers was not near the
top of her form. Despite this, the novel is
remarkable as a treatment of the newly wedded pair
of eccentrics, Lord Peter Wimsey and Harriet Vane,
with Bunter in the offing along with three local
chracters, chiefly comic. Lord Peter's mother,
John Donne, a case of vintage port, and the handling
of "corroded sut," provide plenty of garnishing for
an indifferent murder, even if the reader were not

also given an idea of Lord Peter's powers
under stress.

A2. Clouds of Witness.

London: T. Fisher Unwin, 1926.   315p.
New York: The Dial Press, 1927.   288p.
New York: Harcourt, Brace, 1938.   287p.
New York: Harper, 1955?   287p.
London: New English Library, 1962.   254p.
New York: Avon Books, 1966.   244p.
London: Gollancz, 1969.   320p. (Collected
    stories, v.2)

Three years elapsed between the publication
of Whose Body? (1923) and the Duke of Denver's
case, Clouds of Witness; and after these two
exercises in ingenuity, Miss Sayers never looked
back. Thereafter, almost every year brought
another Lord Peter mystery until she tired of
him. In this second novel, as in her first,
Miss Sayers had to fall back, so to speak, on
the confession of the murderer. There was plenty
of evidence, but no proof, and after this novel
she was not to be caught that way again.

We find Lord Peter in this story confronted
with the problem of his amiable if foolish brother
the Duke of Denver, married to a shrew, Helen,
accused of murder and tried before the House of
Lords, a rare and remarkable occasion. A number
of old friends persist happily, and we have a

chance to meet others, including that correct
solicitor Mr. Murbles. There is even a glimpse
of Denver's son, Peter's young nephew, identified
as "pickled Gherkins." Many years later, in
Gaudy Night, he will become quite devoted to
his chosen "aunt," Harriet Vane. In the present
story, Lord Peter flies across the Atlantic to
make his climactic appearance before the assembled
Lords. The journey was, at that point in time,
no casual event.

James Sandoe indicates that this novel was
reissued in May, 1935 (London: Gollancz) with
"some corrections and amendments" and as preface
"a short biography of Lord Peter Wimsey, brought
up to date... and communicated by his Uncle Paul
Austin Delagardie." The biography also appeared
in reprints of Whose Body?, Unnatural Death, and
The Unpleasantness at the Bellona Club. It was
first published in the United States in 1938 in
the combined edition of The Dawson Pedigree and
Lord Peter Views the Body (New York: Harcourt,
Brace). See (C93).

A3. The Five Red Herrings.

London: Gollancz, 1931.   351p.   (Maps on
        lining papers)
New York: Warren & Putnam, 1931.   398p.
        (Illustrated)
New York: New Avon Library, 1943.   336p.
        (Illustrated)
New York: Harper, 1958.   306p. (Illustrated)
New York: Avon Books, 1968.   286p. (Map)
London: New English Library, 1972.   284p. (Map)

Miss Sayers never did explain why Lord Peter
and his love for Harriet Vane were left dangling
from 1930 to 1932. There is no hint of her in
this novel which was published in the United States
under the title: Suspicious Characters. This story
is not the best Wimsey book and commits the
unpardonable sin in a detective work of being
very dull. It has also dated more than any of the
others and was obviously written to please the
people of Kircudbright, where she lived for a
time and was apparently very happy.

The story concerns the murder of an artist.
His body was found huddled on the pointed rocks
alongside a stream. He might have simply fallen,
but there were too many suspicious elements in
his death, especially when the six prime suspects
had wished him dead. Five of them were red herrings,
but the sixth had cared enough to plot an elaborate

murder scheme which baffled everyone, including
Lord Peter Wimsey.

A4. Gaudy Night.

London: Gollancz, 1935.   483p.
New York: Harcourt, Brace, 1936.   469p.
New York: Harper, 1960.   469p.
London: New English Library, 1963.   447p.
London: Gollancz, 1972.   483p. (Collected
      stories, v.13)

The solving of the mystery created during

the celebration of an Oxford Gaudy provides

the action for this interesting novel. Aside

from the mystery, the psychological problem of

what happens to the ordinarily sensible minds

of a group of women who become suspicious of

each other, is excellently handled. The

characterization is good and the descriptions

of life in a women's college in England during

the period are very interesting. Oxford town

itself stands out quite clearly.

A5. Have His Carcase.

London: Gollancz, 1932.   448p.
New York: Brewer, Warren & Putnam, 1932.   448p.
New York: Pocket Books, 1942.   440p.
New York: Harper, 1959.   448p. (Illustrated)
Harmondsworth ₍Eng₎: Penguin Books, 1962.   360p.
London: Gollancz, 1971.   448p. (Collected
      stories, v.9)
London: New English Library, 1974.   444p.

Harriet Vane finally returns in this novel,

finding a corpse for herself, and playing hard-
to-get with Lord Peter. As Miss Sayers admitted,
these two, having found one another, adamantly
refused, in the independent way of good fictional
characters, to fall into each other's arms.

In the story, a murdered man, an ivory-
handled razor, three hundred pounds in gold coins,
and a coded message are among the ingredients of
a mystery dish that delights the palate of Lord
Peter Wimsey. Generally, this novel is a great
achievement. The people, the motive, the cipher,
and the detection are all well done. Here, too,
is the first (and definitive) use of hemophilia
as a misleading fact. And surely the son, the
mother, and her self-deluded gigolo are definitive
types.

A6. _Murder_ _Must_ _Advertise_; _A_ _Detective_ _Story_.

> London: Gollancz, 1933.   352p.
> New York" Harcourt, Brace, 1933.   344p.
>   (Another issue in this same year includes
>   _Hangman's_ _Holiday_)
> New York: Harper, 1959?   344p.
> London: New English Library, 1962.   256p.
> London: Gollancz, 1971.   352p. (Collected
>   stories, v.10)
> London: New English Library, 1973.   255p.

This novel is a good example of the ability
of Dorothy L. Sayers to get a group of people going.

The advertising agency is inimitable, and,
therefore, better than the DeMomerie crowd that
goes with it. The murder is ingenious and Lord
Peter is just right, but one flaw mars the
criminal scheme: would the postman, after a few
weeks, continue to deliver letters that the
tobacconist declined to accept?

One gets the impression that here Miss
Sayers is playing games with a world (publicity)
that she knew as a paid practitioner. A host of
old friends and acquaintances are present (Lady
Mary is now married to Inspector Parker and Freddy
to Rachel), and there are such new acquaintances
as young Ginger, whose catapult (slingshot) is
vital to the action.

A7. The Nine Tailors; Changes Rung on an Old Theme in
Two Short Touches and Two Full Peals.

London: Gollancz, 1934.   350p. (Illustrated)
New York: Harcourt, Brace, 1934.   331p.
   (Illustrated)
London: Gollancz, 1951.   237p. (Illustrated)
New York: Harcourt, Brace & World, 1962.   311p.
London: Four Square Book, 1965.   255p.
   (Illustrated)
London: Gollancz, 1972.   351p. (Illustrated;
   Collected stories, v.12)
London: New English Library, 1972.   255p.

Known as the campanology novel, this story
further interrupts the Wimsey-Vane affair. Indeed,

by the time Miss Sayers returned to her hero's
love life, she was to discover that he had been
loving one woman for five years without even
having kissed her.

In the story, Lord Peter, driving through a
snow storm one New Year's Eve, goes off the road
near Fenchurch St. Paul, and becomes the over-
night guest of the rector--a providential visit
all around, for Lord Peter, who is well acquainted
with the ancient art of bell-ringing, aids that
night as a substitute. Further than that, he
finds use for his versatile mind later on, at the
shocking discovery of a mutilated corpse in
another man's grave. The unusual plot is developed
with dexterity and ingenuity to a surprising
conclusion.

A8. Strong Poison.

        London: Gollancz, 1930.   288p.
        New York: Brewer & Warren, 1930.   344p.
        New York: Harcourt, Brace, 1936.   252p.
            (Includes Have His Carcase)
        London: Gollancz, 1956.   170p.
        New York: F. Watts, 1958.   252p.
        New York: Harper, 1958.   252p.
        London: Landsborough, 1960.   192p.
        Leicester Eng : Ulverscroft, 1966.   244p.
        London: New English Library, 1968.   192p.
        New York: Avon Books, 1971.

In this novel the reader is introduced to
Harriet Vane who, at the beginning, is on trial
and charged with the arsenic murder of her trying
lover, Philip Boyes. Lord Peter Wimsey is quite
certain that Harriet is innocent, and what
follows proves that he is right. But he is also
in love with Miss Vane, who has no taste for his
pity and refuses him without dashing his hopes
entirely.

What made Miss Sayers suddenly bring love
into the Wimsey stories is not known; it may be
that it just fell in as the story progressed.
Perhaps it was pressure from publishers and fans.
There can be little doubt that Harriet is Dorothy
as she saw herself. Another interesting aspect
of the Sayers method is that she knows how everything is done. None of the men and women in her
books ever have to think twice about picking locks,
opening envelopes while keeping the seals intact,
or stealing wills from under the noses of their
owners.

A9. Unnatural Death.

> London: E. Benn, 1927.   285p.
> New York: The Dial Press, 1928.   299p.
>   (Illustrated)

New York: Harcourt, Brace, 1938.   285p.
    (Also includes: <u>Lord</u> <u>Peter</u> <u>Views</u> <u>the</u> <u>Body</u>)
New York: Harper, 1955.   285p.
London: Gollancz, 1956.   188p.
New York: Avon Books, 1964.   290p.
London: Gollancz, 1969.   285p. (Collected
    stories, v.3)
London: New English Library, 1970.   253p.
London: Gollancz, 1972.   287p. (Illustrated)

The author takes a somewhat different approach
in this novel. She lets the reader know who the
murderer probably is near the beginning, for the
excitement lies in the chase and detection.
In the story a chance remark overheard in a
restaurant starts a long inquiry, and an apparently
natural death is proved to have been murder. The
victims increase in number, as well as in virtue
and attractiveness; hence the crimes become
more and more sinister. Lord Peter, aided by his
friends Inspector Parker and that delightful
maiden lady Miss Climpson, becomes engaged in
very useful, but particularly dangerous work.

The novel was published in the United States
as <u>The</u> <u>Dawson</u> <u>Pedigree</u>.

A10. The <u>Unpleasantness</u> <u>at</u> <u>the</u> <u>Bellona</u> <u>Club</u>.

London: E. Benn, 1928.   287p.
New York: Payson & Clarke, 1928.   345p.
New York: Harper, 1928.   345p. (Reissued
    in 1956?   345p.)

London: New English Library, 1963.   192p.
New York: Avon Books, 1963.   192p.
London: Gollancz, 1969.   285p. (Collected
    stories, v.4)

This is perhaps one of the more satisfying
of the early Wimsey novels. It captures some of
the dreadful sadness and suffering of England
after World War I, where almost an entire
generation was profoundly affected by it. Everyone in the novel constantly alludes to that war,
which never stops happening for them, and they
all seem to be psychologically or physically
afflicted by the terrors of the recent past.

Miss Sayers also describes with a real sense
of verisimilitude--for an outsider anyway--the
stuffy and comic character of a typical English
club. The murder of old General Fentiman fulfills
the punch line of a joke which echoes grotesquely
throughout the book--the one about the denizen of
a club reading his *Times*, who turns out to have
been dead for three days. The villain is that
favorite Sayers nemesis, the man of science, in
this case a brilliant and inhuman physician who,
perhaps because he is a paid-up member of the
Bellona Club, is allowed to shoot himself in (where

alse?), the library, after writing a full
confession.

Lord Peter, who has displayed some of the
compassionate aspects of his character in the
past, now very sweetly effects a cure of Ann
Dorland, a confused young woman who has been
badly treated by a variety of rotten people.
Like a true comic hero, Lord Peter manages to
unite her with the right man at the end of the
book and thus save her from a nervous breakdown.

All. Whose Body?

> London: T. Fisher Unwin, 1923.   278p.
> New York: Boni & Liveright, 1923.   278p.
> London: Collins, 1932.   251p.
> New York: Avon Book Co., 1943.   158p.
> New York: Avon Pub. Co., 1948.   190p.
> New York: Harper, 1956?   252p.
> New York: Avon Books, 1961.   192p.
> London: Gollancz, 1962.   137p.
> London: New English Library, 1968.   191p.
> London: Gollancz, 1971.   288p. (Collected
>   stories, v.1)

As near as can be determined, sometime about
1920, Lord Peter Wimsey was conceived by Dorothy
L. Sayers. She hoped, she has told us, to produce
something "less like a conventional detective
story and more like a novel." Although Lord
Peter did not at first gain the following she
would have liked for him, it was in the decade

after his appearance that the detective novel,
which had labored under a rather shaky
reputation, was to achieve its post-Holmesian
heights. It was clear from the first Sayers
novel that she was able to combine exactness of
detail and authenticity of background with
perception, wit, and humor.

In the story, Lord Peter Wimsey is an amateur
criminologist who pursues his hobby as a sport
out of which he derives considerable amusement.
When a nude corpse, wearing only a golden pince-
nez, is found in the bathtub of the flat of a
timid little architect, and the discovery coincides
with the disappearance of a wealthy financier,
Sir Reuben Levy, whom the body resembled, Lord
Peter's sporting blood is aroused. Together
with a friend from Scotland Yard, he unofficially,
playfully, as it were, conducts a roundabout
inquiry under the jealous eye of the official
Scotland Yard investigators and finally tracks
down the murderer.

James Sandoe indicates that this novel has
an alternate title, noticed in none of the
standard bibliographies, possibly because it

appears in an unusual position (in the Boni &
Liveright edition on 3p. 1.): "The Singular
Adventure of the Man with the Golden Pince-nez."

II. Novels Written in Collaboration with Others

A12. Ask a Policeman.

> London: A. Barker, 1933.   311p. (Illustrated)
> New York: William Morrow, 1933.   311p.
> (Illustrated)

Like The Floating Admiral (A15), this is the
second of three detective novels written by at
least six members of the Detection Club; each
member would write a chapter. The collaborators
in this particular work are: Anthony Berkeley,
Milward Kennedy, Gladys Mitchell, John Rhode,
Dorothy L. Sayers, and Helen Simpson. Miss Sayers
contributed "The Conclusions of Mr. Roger
Sheringham," (pp. 175-225), while Anthony Berkeley
is reporter of "Lord Peter's Privy Council,"
(pp. 226-278).

A13. The Documents in the Case.

> London: E. Benn, 1930.   287p.
> New York: Brewer & Warren, 1930.   304p.
> New York: Avon Books, 1968.   221p.
> London: New English Library, 1969.   204p.

Published in the same year as <u>Strong</u> <u>Poison</u>, this novel did not feature Lord Peter Wimsey. Sayers collaborated with Robert Eustace, the pen-name for Dr. Eustace Robert Barton, M.R.C.S., L.R.C.P., who helped her with the medical details.

In the novel, nothing is concealed from the reader. Each of the characters is revealed in a series of letters and statements which build toward a dramatic climax. The interest of the story lies not so much in the actual crime, but in the analysis of character, the building up of a background, and the genesis of motive, all leading inevitably to the end of poor Mr. Harrison.

A14. <u>Double</u> <u>Death</u>: <u>A</u> <u>Murder</u> <u>Story</u>.

London: Gollancz, 1939.   285p.

This is the third story like <u>The</u> <u>Floating</u> <u>Admiral</u> (A15) and <u>Ask</u> <u>a</u> <u>Policeman</u> (A12), with chapters written by members of the Detection Club. John Chancellor edited this book, and the contributors were: Dorothy L. Sayers, Freeman Wills Crofts, Valentine Williams, F. Tennyson Jesse, Anthony Armstrong, and David Hume.

A15. The Floating Admiral.

>London: Hodder & Stoughton, 1931.   351p.
>Garden City, N.Y.: Published for the Crime
>   Club, Inc. by Doubleday, Doran, 1932.
>   309p. (Illustrated)

A story with chapters written by certain

members of the Detection Club, including: G.K.

Chesterton, Canon Victor L. Whitechurch, G.D.H.

and M. Cole, Henry Wade, Agatha Christie, John

Rhode, Milward Kennedy, Dorothy L. Sayers, Ronald

A. Knox, Freeman Wills Crofts, Edgar Jepson,

Clemence Dane, and Anthony Berkeley. Miss Sayers

contributed the "Introduction" (pp.1-5), Chapter

VII, "Shocks for the Inspector" (pp.92-128), and

her solution to the crime (pp.275-295).

III. Collections

A16. The Lord Peter Omnibus.

>London: Gollancz, 1964.   549p.

Includes the following novels: Clouds of

Witness (A2); Unnatural Death (A9); and The

Unpleasantness at the Bellona Club (A10).

A17. The New Sayers Omnibus.

>London: Gollancz, 1956.   244, 307, 246p.
>   (Illustrated)

Includes the following novels: <u>The</u> <u>Five</u>
<u>Red</u> <u>Herrings</u> (A3); <u>Have</u> <u>His</u> <u>Carcase</u> (A5); and
<u>Murder</u> <u>Must</u> <u>Advertise</u> (A6).

A18. <u>Omnibus</u>.

New York: Harcourt, Brace, 1937.   252, 345, 398p.

Includes the following novels: <u>Whose</u> <u>Body</u>? (All);
<u>The</u> <u>Unpleasantness</u> <u>at</u> <u>the</u> <u>Bellona</u> <u>Club</u> (A10); and
<u>Suspicious</u> <u>Characters</u>, i.e., <u>The</u> <u>Five</u> <u>Red</u> <u>Herrings</u> (A3).

A19. <u>The</u> <u>Sayers</u> <u>Holiday</u> <u>Book</u>.

London: Gollancz, 1963.   696p.

Includes the following novels and collections
of short stories: <u>Gaudy</u> <u>Night</u> (A4); <u>Strong</u> <u>Poison</u> (A8);
and <u>In</u> <u>the</u> <u>Teeth</u> <u>of</u> <u>the</u> <u>Evidence</u> (B46).

A20. <u>The</u> <u>Sayers</u> <u>Tandem</u>.

London: Gollancz, 1967.   237, 295p. (First
published in 1957)

Includes the following novels: <u>The</u> <u>Nine</u> <u>Tailors</u>
(A7); and <u>Busman's</u> <u>Honeymoon</u> (A1).

A21. <u>Three</u> <u>for</u> <u>Lord</u> <u>Peter</u> <u>Wimsey</u>.

New York: Harper & Row, 1966?   530p.

Includes the following novels: <u>Whose</u> <u>Body</u>? (All);
<u>Clouds</u> <u>of</u> <u>Witness</u> (A2); and <u>Unnatural</u> <u>Death</u> (A9).

A22. <u>3</u> <u>Lord</u> <u>Peter</u> <u>Mysteries</u>.

New York: Harcourt, Brace, 19--?   398p.
(Illustrated)

Includes the following novels: <u>Whose</u> <u>Body</u>? (A11); <u>The</u> <u>Unpleasantness</u> <u>at</u> <u>the</u> <u>Bellona</u> <u>Club</u> (A10); and <u>Suspicious</u> <u>Characters</u>, i.e., <u>The</u> <u>Five</u> <u>Red</u> <u>Herrings</u> (A3).

Section B

SHORT STORIES

The quality of the short stories written by
Dorothy L. Sayers can be termed uneven. But cannot
this be said of most writers of this genre? More
important, though, is the fact that she wrote good
English--a rare quality among detective writers. She
possessed a fine sense of humor and a genius for
creating the most unexpected situations. She infused
most of her tales with intelligent perception and a
certain vivacity of observation. With her own stories
she is more dependent on mere story telling, and shows
that she can do it, though the reader might become
weary if the tales had been spun out at greater length.

Most detective fiction readers are unaware that
between 1933 and 1935, Miss Sayers turned detective-
story critic and wrote a series of weekly reviews for
the London Sunday Times. The adjective most often used
to characterize her private-eye perception has been
"remarkable." For instance, she recalls that many
readers of detective novels are supposed to have

"a prejudice against detective stories. Yet the
world's greatest reputation in detective stories was
built upon the short story. There are only four full-
length Sherlock Holmes novels: the rest of that
enormous fame is a short story achievement." She
is quoted as saying "plot is not everything, style
is not everything; only by combining them can we get
a detective story that is also good literature."

Many have felt that Dorothy L. Sayers did more
to add literary tone to crime fiction than did most
of her contemporaries, and it is to her infinite credit
that she attempted to wed the detective story to the
legitimate novel of manners with utmost deliberation--
almost, it might be said, with malice aforethought.

For the purpose of organization, this section
is divided into four parts. The first is an alphabetical
listing of each short story by original title. Below
the title a brief statement about the story is given
followed by the source or sources in which it has
appeared. The second part is an alphabetical listing
of short stories written by Miss Sayers that appeared
as collections. The third part lists collections of
short stories written by others but edited by Sayers.
Part four is an alphabetical list of anthologies and

periodicals in which short stories appeared. All of these parts are cross-referenced for convenience in locating individual stories or sources.

I. Individual Short Stories

  B1. The Abominable History of the Man with Copper Fingers.

       In the story an electro-plating artist provides Lord Peter Wimsey and an American actor with a great shock. This short story has appeared in:

        Hitchcock - Alfred Hitchcock Presents Stories not for the Nervous (B88).

        Sayers - Lord Peter; a Collection... (B47).

        -----. - Lord Peter Views the Body (B48).

        -----. - A Treasury of Sayers Stories (B50).

  B2. Absolutely Elsewhere.

       Mr. Grimbold's murder could not have been committed by anyone according to the immediate evidence. Lord Peter Wimsey, by means of his superlative deductive expertise, is able to discover who did it. This story has appeared in:

Green - Ten Tales of Detection (B81).

Mystery; the Illustrated Detective Magazine

(B100), under the title:"Impossible Alibi."

Sayers - In the Teeth of the Evidence (B46).

-----. - Lord Peter; a Collection... (B47).

B3. The Adventurous Exploit of the Cave of Ali Baba.

In the story Lord Peter Wimsey does--or does he? A secret society discovers that it has an ingenious traitor among its membership. This story has appeared in:

Bauer - Short Stories in Parallel (B60).

Ernst - Favorite Sleuths (B74).

Haycraft - Boy's Second Book of Great Detective

Stories (B83).

Richardson - Best Mystery Stories (B106).

Sayers - Great Short Stories of Detection,

Mystery and Horror, 2d Series (B52).

-----. - Lord Peter; a Collection... (B47).

-----. - Lord Peter Views the Body (B48).

-----. - A Treasury of Sayers Stories (B50).

B4. An Arrow O'er the House.

Some advertising used to arouse certain expectations backfires. This story has appeared in:

Sayers - In the Teeth of the Evidence (B46).

B5. The Bibulous Business of a Matter of Taste.

There is some question as to which man is
the real Lord Peter Wimsey. The taste of wine
tells the tale. This story has appeared in:

Crime and Detection (B67).

Ellery Queen's Mystery Magazine (B73).

Fadiman - Dionysus (B76).

-----. - The Joys of Wine (B77).

Queen - 101 Years' Entertainment (B103).

Sayers - Lord Peter; a Collection... (B47).

-----. - Lord Peter Views the Body (B48).

-----. - A Treasury of Sayers Stories (B50).

B6. Bitter Almonds.

Montague Egg, with his superlative knowledge
of wine, brings a surprising verdict in a case of
unexpected death. This story has appeared in:

Sayers - In the Teeth of the Evidence (B46).

B7. Blood Sacrifice.

Mr. Garrick Drury, a famous actor, made the
play a financial success, but the playwright
thought his final act the best. This story has
appeared in:

Queen - <u>Rogue's Gallery</u> (B104).

Sayers - <u>In the Teeth of the Evidence</u> (B46).

<u>Six Against the Yard</u> (B110).

B8. <u>The Cyprian Cat</u>.

A man with a fear of cats, and a feline woman combine to create a baffling mystery. This story has appeared in:

Costain - <u>More Stories to Remember</u> (B66).

Karloff - <u>And the Darkness Falls</u> (B91).

Margolies - <u>Strange and Fantastic Stories</u> (B96).

<u>My Best Thriller</u> (B98).

Sayers - <u>In the Teeth of the Evidence</u> (B46).

Spectorsky - <u>Man into Beast</u> (B111).

B9. <u>Dilemma</u>.

In the story, human judgement in crises make two stories and a vindication. This story has appeared in:

Sayers - <u>In the Teeth of the Evidence</u> (B46).

B10. <u>Dirt Cheap</u>.

Mr. Pringle, a jewellry salesman, is murdered and robbed. Everyone had an alibi, even Mr. Montague Egg. The answer to this baffling crime lies in the chiming of a clock which Monty discovers has a mysterious counterpart. This story has appeared in:

Sayers - <u>In the Teeth of the Evidence</u> (B46).

B11. The Entertaining Episode of the Article in
      Question.

    Lord Peter's quick ear changes his direction
of travel and gives an interesting end to a
wedding party. This story has appeared in:

    Ferguson - Theme and Variation in the Short
        Story (B78).

    MacGowan - Sleuths (B94).

    Sayers - Lord Peter; a Collection... (B47).

    -----. - Lord Peter Views the Body (B48).

    -----. - A Treasury of Sayers Stories (B50).

B12. False Weight.

    A traveling salesman is suspected of killing
another. Mr. Montague Egg discovers that the
weights of a clock are an important clue, and
that a missing key points directly to the person
or persons responsible. This story has appeared in:

    Sayers - In the Teeth of the Evidence (B46).

B13. The Fantastic Horror of the Cat in the Bag.

    A speedy chase in pursuit of a man who dropped
a satchel has some surprising results. This story
has appeared in:

Sayers - <u>Lord</u> <u>Peter</u>; <u>a</u> <u>Collection</u>... (B47).

-----. - <u>Lord</u> <u>Peter</u> <u>Views</u> <u>the</u> <u>Body</u> (B48).

-----. - <u>A</u> <u>Treasury</u> <u>of</u> <u>Sayers</u> <u>Stories</u> (B50).

B14. <u>The</u> <u>Fascinating</u> <u>Problem</u> <u>of</u> <u>Uncle</u> <u>Meleager's</u> <u>Will</u>.

A crossword puzzle gives a clue to a hiding place for a will. This story has appeared in:

Sayers - <u>Lord</u> <u>Peter</u>; <u>a</u> <u>Collection</u>... (B47).

-----. - <u>Lord</u> <u>Peter</u> <u>Views</u> <u>the</u> <u>Body</u> (B48).

-----. - <u>A</u> <u>Treasury</u> <u>of</u> <u>Sayers</u> <u>Stories</u> (B50)

B15. <u>The</u> <u>Fountain</u> <u>Plays</u>.

In the story we find a tale of blackmail and an exchange of masters. This story has appeared in:

Lee - <u>Murder</u> <u>Mixture</u> (B93).

Sayers - <u>Hangman's</u> <u>Holiday</u> (B45).

-----. - <u>A</u> <u>Treasury</u> <u>of</u> <u>Sayers</u> <u>Stories</u> (B50).

B16. <u>The</u> <u>Haunted</u> <u>Policeman</u>.

Policeman P.C. Burt hears a murder being committed and views the aftermath through a mailbox; however, the whole scene mysteriously vanishes before he gains entrance to the house. Lord Peter, who has just become a father, takes pity on the perplexed officer and sets out to solve the mystery. This story has appeared in:

Detection Medley (B71).

Ellery Queen's Mystery Magazine (B73).

Harper's Bazaar (B82).

Sayers - Lord Peter; a Collection... (B47).

-----. - Striding Folly (B49).

Strand Magazine (B112).

Street - Line-up (B113).

B17. The Image in the Mirror.

A surprising reflection, or lack of it, gives a strange twist to this tale. This story has appeared in:

Ellery Queen's Mystery Magazine (B73).

Sayers - Hangman's Holiday (B45).

-----. - Lord Peter; a Collection... (B47).

-----. - Tales of Detection (B58).

-----. - A Treasury of Sayers Stories (B50).

Also published as a pamphlet (G66).

B18. In the Teeth of the Evidence.

A charred body is identified by dental records and suicide is suspected. Lord Peter is not convinced and a re-examination provides a murderous conclusion. This story has appeared in:

Cuppy - Murder Without Tears (B68).

Haycraft - Three Times Three, Mystery Omnibus (B86).

Sayers - In the Teeth of the Evidence (B46).

-----. - Lord Peter; a Collection... (B47).

B19. The Incredible Elopement of Lord Peter Wimsey.

A beautiful young woman is apparently exiled in one of the most forlorn corners of the world because it was believed that she was bewitched. This is perhaps the queerest case that Lord Peter Wimsey ever investigated; but then, as Lord Peter himself said, "I am always interested in queer things." This story has appeared in:

Ellery Queen's Mystery Magazine (B73). Published under the title: "The Power of Darkness."

Sayers - Hangman's Holiday (B45).

-----. - Lord Peter; a Collection... (B47).

-----. - A Treasury of Sayers Stories (B50).

Also published as a pamphlet (G67).

B20. The Inspiration of Mr. Budd.

In the story, "knowledge is power," thought Mr. Budd, and in this case his knowledge gave him a new business. This story has appeared in:

Daly - My Favorite Suspense Stories (B70).

Dickinson - The Case of the Vanishing Spinster (B72).

My Best Detective Story (B97).

Postgate - Detective Stories of Today (B102).

Sayers - In the Teeth of the Evidence (B46).

Shibata - The Confession and Two Other Stories (B109).

B21. The Learned Adventure of the Dragon's Head.

Latin and book collecting lead to a treasure
hunt. This story has appeared in:

Bond - Famous stories of code and cipher (B64).

Haycraft - Ten Great Mysteries (B85).

Manley - Grande Dames of Detection (B95).

Queen - Sporting Blood (B105).

Sayers - Lord Peter; a Collection... (B47).

-----. - Lord Peter Views the Body (B48).

-----. - A Treasury of Sayers Stories (B50).

Ordean Hagen (I4) on p.336, indicates this was
published in pamphlet form--London: Watkins, 1928.??

B22. The Leopard Lady.

In the story a mysterious company helps some
heirs. This story has appeared in:

Ellery Queen's Mystery Magazine (B73).

Sayers - In the Teeth of the Evidence (B46).

B23. Maher-Shalal-Hashbaz.

Monty Egg rescues a girl's cat not realizing
what consequences follow. This story has appeared in:

Sayers - Hangman's Holiday (B45).

-----. - A Treasury of Sayers Stories (B50).

B24. The Man Who Knew How.

      This is the chilling story of a man who
lived in terror of a merciless killer who seemed
to follow him as closely as his shadow. This story
has appeared in:

      Ellery Queen's Mystery Magazine (B73).

      Grand Magazine (B80).

      Hitchcock - Alfred Hitchcock's Spellbinders
         in Suspense (B89).

      Sayers - Hangman's Holiday (B45).

      -----. - A Treasury of Sayers Stories (B50).

B25. The Milk-Bottles.

      Mr. Hector Puncheon, of the Morning Star,
writes a breezy half-column about milk-bottles.
This leads to a mystery about some milk-bottles
left by a quarreling couple that smacks of murder.
When the police finally open the door they meet
with a startling surprise. The story has appeared
in:

      Nash's Magazine (B101).

      Sayers - In the Teeth of the Evidence (B46).

B26. Murder at Penetecost.

      Montague Egg penetrates the Bodleian Library

in search of a cunning murderer. This story
has appeared in:

    Sayers - <u>Hangman's</u> <u>Holiday</u> (B45).

    -----. - <u>A</u> <u>Treasury</u> <u>of</u> <u>Sayers</u> <u>Stories</u> (B50).

B27. <u>Murder</u> <u>in</u> <u>the</u> <u>Morning</u>.

    For a few minutes, things look black for
Montague Egg, but time proves him innocent. This
story has appeared in:

    Sayers - <u>Hangman's</u> <u>Holiday</u> (B45).

    -----. - <u>A</u> <u>Treasury</u> <u>of</u> <u>Sayers</u> <u>Stories</u> (B50).

B28. <u>Nebuchadnezzar</u>.

    Charades and a vivid imagination lead a
butler to leap to a wrong conclusion. This
story has appeared in:

    Sayers - <u>In</u> <u>the</u> <u>Teeth</u> <u>of</u> <u>the</u> <u>Evidence</u> (B46).

B29. <u>The</u> <u>Necklace</u> <u>of</u> <u>Pearls</u>.

    A valuable necklace of pearl is ingeniously
hidden during the Christmas season. This story
has appeared in:

    <u>Ellery</u> <u>Queen's</u> <u>Mystery</u> <u>Magazine</u> (B73).

    Sayers - <u>Hangman's</u> <u>Holiday</u> (B45).

    -----. - <u>Lord</u> <u>Peter</u>; <u>a</u> <u>Collection</u>... (B47).

    -----. - <u>A</u> <u>Treasury</u> <u>of</u> <u>Sayers</u> <u>Stories</u> (B50).

B30. <u>One</u> <u>Too</u> <u>Many</u>.

Montague Egg shows the inspector how two men can be three and ride on one ticket. This story has appeared in:

Sayers - <u>Hangman's</u> <u>Holiday</u> (B45).

B31. <u>The</u> <u>Piscatorial</u> <u>Farce</u> <u>of</u> <u>the</u> <u>Stolen</u> <u>Stomach</u>.

In the story there is a strange will where an eccentric old man leaves his alimentary tract to his great nephew. This story has appeared in:

Sayers - <u>Lord</u> <u>Peter</u>; <u>a</u> <u>Collection</u>... (B47).

-----. - <u>Lord</u> <u>Peter</u> <u>Views</u> <u>the</u> <u>Body</u> (B48).

-----. - <u>A</u> <u>Treasury</u> <u>of</u> <u>Sayers</u> <u>Stories</u> (B50).

<u>Senior</u> <u>Scholastic</u>. <u>Teachers</u> <u>Edition</u>. (B108).

B32. <u>The</u> <u>Poisoned</u> <u>Dow</u> <u>'08.</u>

It takes a wine dealer, such as Montague Egg, to know a bottle inside and out. This story has appeared in:

<u>Ellery</u> <u>Queen's</u> <u>Mystery</u> <u>Magazine</u> (B73).

Sayers - <u>Hangman's</u> <u>Holiday</u> (B45).

-----. - <u>A</u> <u>Treasury</u> <u>of</u> <u>Sayers</u> <u>Stories</u> (B50).

B33. <u>The</u> <u>Professor's</u> <u>Manuscript</u>.

Montague Egg visits a prospective customer, one Professor Pindar. The Professor's library

leads Monty to some interesting conclusions
about this strange little man. This story has
appeared in:

>Barzun - The Delights of Detection (B59).
>
>Berbich - Stories of Crime and Detection (B63).
>
>Sayers - In the Teeth of the Evidence (B46).

B34. The Queen's Square.

An evening's entertainment with all the guests
dressed as games leads to a sad but colorful
ending. This story has appeared in:

>Ellery Queen's Mystery Magazine (B73).
>
>Sayers - Hangman's Holiday (B45).
>
>-----. - Lord Peter; a Collection... (B47).
>
>-----. - A Treasury of Sayers Stories (B50).

B35. Scrawns.

A new servant girl is frightened by strange
grave digging in the night. This story has
appeared in:

>Kahn - The Edge of the Chair (B90).
>
>Sayers - In the Teeth of the Evidence (B46).

B36. A Shot at Goal.

Mr. Robbins, a member of the Twiddleton
Football Committee meets with foul play. By

knowing the habits of a certain profession,
Monty Egg alerts the police to the right clue.
This story has appeared in:

Sayers - In the Teeth of the Evidence (B46).

B37. Sleuths on the Scent.

In the story a man's profession gives him
away. This story has appeared in:

Sayers - Hangman's Holiday (B45).

-----. - A Treasury of Sayers Stories (B50).

B38. Striding Folly.

In the story a Mr. Mellilow exhibits his skill
as a chess player. His opponents, however, were
not always of the highest character. One of them
is murdered and he is suspected. He is saved to
some extent by a strange dream which Lord Peter
Wimsey sees as providential. This story has
appeared in:

Detection Medley (B71).

Ellery Queen's Mystery Magazine (B73).

Sayers - Lord Peter; a Collection... (B47).

-----. - Striding Folly (B49).

Street - Line-up (B113).

B39. <u>Suspicion</u>.

With regard to this tale, it would ruin the appetite if one suspected his cook of being a poisoner. This story has appeared in:

<u>Bedside</u> <u>Tales</u> (B61).

Bond - <u>Handbook</u> <u>for</u> <u>Poisoners</u> (B65).

Cuppy - <u>World's</u> <u>Great</u> <u>Mystery</u> <u>Stories</u> (B69).

<u>Ellery</u> <u>Queen's</u> <u>Mystery</u> <u>Magazine</u> (B73).

Evans - <u>The</u> <u>Horizontal</u> <u>Reader</u> (B75).

Kimball - <u>Short</u> <u>Story</u> <u>Reader</u> (B92).

<u>Mystery</u> <u>League</u> <u>Magazine</u> (B99).

Queen - <u>101</u> <u>Years'</u> <u>Entertainment</u> (B103).

Sandrus - <u>Famous</u> <u>Mysteries</u> (B107).

Sayers - <u>In</u> <u>the</u> <u>Teeth</u> <u>of</u> <u>the</u> <u>Evidence</u> (B46).

Wise - <u>Great</u> <u>Tales</u> <u>of</u> <u>Terror</u> <u>and</u> <u>the</u> <u>Supernatural</u>
(B115).

B40. <u>Talboys</u>.

Local rivalry over a village flower show, one of Lord Peter's children accused of theft, and something nasty in the furnace room, combine to make an amusing tale. This story has appeared in:

Sayers - <u>Lord</u> <u>Peter</u>; <u>a</u> <u>Collection</u>... (B47).

-----. - <u>Striding</u> <u>Folly</u> (B49).

B41. The <u>Undignified</u> <u>Melodrama</u> <u>of</u> <u>the</u> <u>Bone</u> <u>of</u>
<u>Contention</u>.

A silent ghostly coach with headless horses
and coachman have a surprising meaning.   This
story has appeared in:

Haycraft - <u>Fourteen</u> <u>Great</u> <u>Detective</u> <u>Stories</u> B84).

-----.   - <u>A</u> <u>Treasury</u> <u>of</u> <u>Great</u> <u>Mysteries</u> (B87).

Sayers - <u>Lord</u> <u>Peter</u>; <u>a</u> <u>Collection</u>... (B47).

-----. - <u>Lord</u> <u>Peter</u> <u>Views</u> <u>the</u> <u>Body</u> (B48).

-----. - <u>A</u> <u>Treasury</u> <u>of</u> <u>Sayers</u> <u>Stories</u> (B50).

B42. The <u>Unprincipled</u> <u>Affair</u> <u>of</u> <u>the</u> <u>Practical</u> <u>Joker</u>.

Lord Peter turns the tables on a diamond
thief by means of a friendly poker game. This
story has appeared in:

Sayers - <u>Lord</u> <u>Peter</u>; <u>a</u> <u>Collection</u> (B47).

-----. - <u>Lord</u> <u>Peter</u> <u>Views</u> <u>the</u> <u>Body</u> (B48).

-----. - <u>A</u> <u>Treasury</u> <u>of</u> <u>Sayers</u> <u>Stories</u> (B50).

B43. The <u>Unsolved</u> <u>Puzzle</u> <u>of</u> <u>the</u> <u>Man</u> <u>with</u> <u>No</u> <u>Face</u>.

A murdered man with his face badly disfigured
is found on a beach. Lord Peter produces some
good theories about the crime, but perhaps the
answer to the puzzle lies within a fairy story,
not another man's confession. This story has

appeared in:

> Sayers - <u>Lord</u> <u>Peter</u>; <u>a</u> <u>Collection</u>... (B47).
>
> -----. - <u>Lord</u> <u>Peter</u> <u>Views</u> <u>the</u> <u>Body</u> (B48).
>
> -----. - <u>A</u> <u>Treasury</u> <u>of</u> <u>Sayers</u> <u>Stories</u> (B50).

Also published as a pamphlet (G74).

B44. The <u>Vindictive</u> <u>Story</u> <u>of</u> <u>the</u> <u>Footsteps</u> <u>that</u> <u>Ran</u>.

Mr. Brotherton's wife had apparently been stabbed to death by a jealous lover, but Lord Peter is suspicious about a roasting chicken that holds the key to this crime. This story has appeared in:

> <u>Ellery</u> <u>Queen's</u> <u>Mystery</u> <u>Magazine</u> (B73).
>
> Sayers - <u>Lord</u> <u>Peter</u>; <u>a</u> <u>Collection</u>... (B47).
>
> -----. - <u>Lord</u> <u>Peter</u> <u>Views</u> <u>the</u> <u>Body</u> (B48).
>
> -----. - <u>A</u> <u>Treasury</u> <u>of</u> <u>Sayers</u> <u>Stories</u> (B50).

II. <u>Collections</u> <u>of</u> <u>Short</u> <u>Stories</u>

B45. <u>Hangman's</u> <u>Holiday</u>.

> London: Gollancz, 1933.   288p.   (Illustrated)
> New York: Harcourt, Brace, 1933.   282p.
> Harmondsworth [Eng.]: Penguin, 1962.   192p.
> New York: Avon Books, 1969.   191p.
> London: Gollancz, 1971.   288p.   (Collected
>   stories, v.11)

This collection of short stories contains four

Peter Wimsey tales, six Montague Egg, and two others. Montague Egg, wine salesman, Miss Sayers' other detective, being strictly commercial and lower middle-class, has a charm of his own wholly different from Lord Peter's. While he does not irritate, neither does he entrance. Perhaps Miss Sayers was trying, among other things, to make use of the knowledge of wines and spirits she had got up (one supposes) for Lord Peter's sake.

Contents:--The image in the mirror (B17).-- The incredible elopement of Lord Peter Wimsey (B19). --The queen's square (B34).--The necklace of pearls (B29).--The poisoned Dow '08 (B32).-- Sleuths on the scent (B37).--Murder in the morning (B27).--One too many (B30).--Murder at Pentecost (B26).--Maher-shalal-hashbaz (B23).-- The man who knew how (B24).--The fountain plays (B15).

B46. In the Teeth of the Evidence, and Other Stories.

London: Gollancz, 1939.   286p.
New York: Harcourt, Brace, 1940.   311p.
New York: New Avon Library, 1943.   225p.
London: Landsborough, 1960.   220p.
London: New English Library, 1961.   220p.
New York: Avon Books, 1967.   221p.
London: Gollancz, 1972.   355p. (Collected
    stories, v.15)

A collection of stories of detection, some of

which have been previously published in
magazines. Two stories are about Lord Peter
Wimsey, and five about Montague Egg. These
stories vary in their quality, and they
usually have little twists in their tails.

Contents:--In the teeth of the evidence (B18).
--Absolutely elsewhere (B2).--A shot at goal (B36).
--Dirt cheap (B10).--Bitter almonds (B6).--
False weight (B12).--The professor's manuscript
(B33).--The milk-bottles (B25).--Dilemma (B9).--
An arrow o'er the house (B4).--Scrawns (B35).--
Nebuchadnezzar (B28).--The inspiration of Mr.
Budd (B20).--Blood sacrifice (B7).--Suspicion
(B39).--The leopard lady (B22).--The Cyprian cat
(B8).

B47. Lord Peter; A Collection of All the Lord Peter
Wimsey Stories.

New York: Harper & Row, 1972.   487p.
New York: Avon Books, 1972.   487p.

Compiled and with an introduction by James
Sandoe. Coda by Carolyn Heilbrun and Codetta by
E.C. Bentley.

Contents:--The abominable history of the man
with copper fingers (B1).--The entertaining

episode of the article in question (B11).--
The fascinating problem of Uncle Meleager's
will (B14).--The fantastic horror of the cat in
the bag (B13).--The unprincipled affair of the
practical joker (B42).--The undignified melodrama
of the bone of contention (B41).--The vindictive
story of the footsteps that ran (B44).--The
bibulous business of a matter of taste (B5).--
The learned adventure of the dragon's head (B21).
--The piscatorial farce of the stolen stomach
(B31).--The unsolved puzzle of the man with no
face (B43).--The adventurous exploit of the cave
of Ali Baba (B3).--The image in the mirror (B17).
--The incredible elopement of Lord Peter Wimsey
(B19).--The queen's square (B34).--The necklace
of pearls (B29).--In the teeth of the evidence
(B18).--Absolutely elsewhere (B2).--Striding
folly (B38).--The haunted policeman (B16).--
Talboys (B40).   Coda: Sayers, Lord Peter, and
God, by Carolyn Heilbrun (H5). Codetta: Greedy
night, a parody, by E.C. Bentley (H16).

B48. Lord Peter Views the Body.

>London: Gollancz, 1928.   317p.
>New York: Brewer & Warren, 1929.   317p.
>Harmondsworth ʳEng.ᒈ : Penguin, 1962.   281p.
>New York: Avon Books, 1969.   255p.
>London: New English Library, 1974.   288p.

This is a collection of twelve short stories
which had been previously published in several
periodicals. It is Miss Sayers' prime collection.
The stories are not equally fine, but so many
are--even the melodramatic one at the end--that
it would be difficult to locate a rival entry in
a competition for variety, balance, picturesqueness,
and sheer ability to handle detective ideas, let
alone invent them. Most of the stories stress
the fantastic, grotesque and macabre.

Contents:--The abominable history of the
man with copper fingers (B1).--The entertaining
episode of the article in question (B11).-- The
fascinating problem of Uncle Meleager's will (B14).
--The fantastic horror of the cat in the bag (B13).
--The unrpincipled affair of the practical joker
(B42).--The undignified melodrama of the bone
of contention (B41).--The vindictive story of
the footsteps that ran (B44).--The bibulous

business of a matter of taste (B5).--The
learned adventure of the dragon's head (B21).
--The piscatorial farce of the stolen stomach
(B31).--The unsolved puzzle of the man with no
face (B43).--The adventurous exploit of the cave
of Ali Baba (B3).

B49. Striding Folly, Including Three Final Lord Peter
Wimsey Stories.

London: New English Library, 1972.   124p.
(Illustrated)

A collection of three of Sayers' short
stories. Aside from "Striding Folly" (B38),
included are "The Haunted Policeman," (B16),
and "Talboys," (B40). The introductory essay
was written by Janet Hitchman.

B50. A Treasury of Sayers Stories.

London: Gollancz, 1958; 1967.   347p.
(Illustrated)

A collection of 24 of her short stories.

Contents:--The image in the mirror (B17).--
The incredible elopement of Lord Peter Wimsey
(B19).--The queen's square (B34).--The necklace
of pearls (B29).--The poisoned Dow '08 (B32).--
Sleuths on the scent (B37).--Murder in the
morning (B27).--Murder at Pentecost (B26).--

Maher-shalal-hashbaz (B23).--The man who knew
how (B24).--The fountain plays (B15).--The
abominable history of the man with copper
fingers (B1).--The entertaining episode of the
article in question (B11).--The fascinating
problem of Uncle Meleager's will (B14).--The
fantastic horror of the cat in the bag (B13).--
The unprincipled affair of the practical joker
(B42).--The undignified melodrama of the bone
of contention (B41).--The vindictive story of
the footsteps that ran (B44).--The bibulous
business of a matter of taste (B5).--The learned
adventure of the dragon's head (B21).--The
piscatorial farce of the stolen stomach (B31).--
The unsolved puzzle of the man with no face
(B43).--The adventurous exploit of the cave of
Ali Baba (B3).

III. Collections of Short Stories Written by Others and
Edited by Dorothy L. Sayers

B51. Great Short Stories of Detection, Mystery and
Horror.
London: Gollancz, 1928.   1229p.

This was the first of three collections of short stories compiled by Miss Sayers, and it includes her excellent essay on the history and growth of detective fiction as the Introduction. This first collection was published in the United States as <u>The Omnibus of Crime</u>, though form and content vary between the many British and U.S. editions of the series (see B54).

B52. <u>Great Short Stories of Detection, Mystery and Horror, Second Series</u>.

London: Gollancz, 1931.   1147p.

In the Introduction to this collection Miss Sayers predicted a trend toward the psychological novel which proved to be a major development in crime fiction during the decades of the 1930's and 1940's. Published in the United States as <u>The Second Omnibus of Crime</u> (B55). Includes the short story: "The Adventurous Exploit of the Cave of Ali Baba," (B3).

B53. <u>Great Short Stories of Detection, Mystery and Horror, Third Series</u>.

London: Gollancz, 1934.   1069p.

Included in this collection are twenty-one

detective and mystery stories, and thirty-one
mystery and horror stories. Miss Sayers provides
a short introduction. Published in the United
States as The Third Omnibus of Crime (B56).

B54. The Omnibus of Crime.

New York: Payson & Clarke, 1929.   1177p.
New York: Harcourt, Brace, 1929.   920p.

Published in Great Britain as Great Short
Stories of Detection, Mystery and Horror; see
(B51). As an example of content variation
between this and a later Gollancz edition, three
stories will be found in the British edition
which are not included in the U.S. edition;
however, the U.S. edition has one story which
the British edition doesn't have.

B55. The Second Omnibus of Crime.

New York: Coward-McCann, 1932.   855p.

Originally published in Britain, this U.S.
edition contains fifty-two short stories, while
the British edition contains sixty-seven.
See (B52) for additional notes.

B56. The Third Omnibus of Crime.

New York: Coward-McCann, 1935.   808p.
See (B53) for annotation.

B57. Stories of the Supernatural, from the Omnibus
of Crime.

New York: MacFadden-Bartell, 1963.   144p.

A collection of the more interesting stories
contained in The Omnibus of Crime.

B58. Tales of Detection.

London: J.M. Dent & Sons, 1936.   382p.
(Everyman's Library, no. 928)

This collection includes stories by Poe,
Christie, Wilkie Collins, G.K. Chesterton,
Robert Eustace, Anthony Berkeley, and others.
Contains also her short story: "Image in the
Mirror," (B17), pp. 266-290. The Introduction
is considered by many to be a work of rare
insight and judgement.

IV. Anthologies and Periodicals Containing Short Stories
by Dorothy L. Sayers

B59. Barzun, Jacques, ed. The Delights of Detection.

New York: Criterion Books, 1961.   381p.

Includes the short story: "The Professor's
Manuscript," (B33).

B60. Bauer, William F., ed. <u>Short</u> <u>Stories</u> <u>in</u> <u>Parallel</u>.
Compiled with W. Paul Bowden. Boston:
D.C. Heath, 1942.   462p.
Includes the short story: "The Adventurous
Exploit of the Cave of Ali Baba," (B3).

B61. <u>The</u> <u>Bedside</u> <u>Tales</u>, <u>a</u> <u>Gay</u> <u>Collection</u>. With an
introduction by Peter Arno. New York:
Wm. Penn Pub. Corp., 1945.   569p.
Includes the short story: "Suspicion," (B39).

B62. Bentley, Edmund C. <u>The</u> <u>Second</u> <u>Century</u> <u>of</u>
<u>Detective</u> <u>Stories</u>. London: Hutchinson,
1938?   761p.
According to: <u>A</u> <u>Catalogue</u> <u>of</u> <u>Crime</u> (p.462),
Miss Sayers is represented in this work. (See H15).

B63. Berbrich, Joan D., comp. <u>Stories</u> <u>of</u> <u>Crime</u> <u>and</u>
<u>Detection</u>. New York: McGraw-Hill, 1974.
296p.
Includes the short story: "The Professor's
Manuscript," (B33).

B64. Bond, Raymond T., ed. <u>Famous</u> <u>Stories</u> <u>of</u> <u>Code</u> <u>and</u>
<u>Cipher</u>. New York: Rinehart, 1947.   342p.
Includes the short story: "The Learned
Adventure of the Dragon's Head," (B21).

B65. Bond, Raymond T., ed. <u>Handbook</u> <u>for</u> <u>Poisoners</u>;
     <u>A</u> <u>Collection</u> <u>of</u> <u>Famous</u> <u>Poison</u> <u>Stories</u>,
     <u>with</u> <u>an</u> <u>Introduction</u> <u>on</u> <u>Poisons</u>. New York:
     Rinehart, 1951.   311p.
     Includes the short story: "Suspicion," (B39).

B66. Costain, Thomas B., ed. <u>More</u> <u>Stories</u> <u>to</u> <u>Remember</u>.
     With John Beecroft. Illus. by Frederick E.
     Banbery. Garden City, N.Y.: Doubleday, 1958.
     2v.
     Includes the short story: "The Cyprian
     Cat," (B8).

B67. <u>Crime</u> <u>and</u> <u>Detection</u>. Oxford: Oxford University
     Press, 1930.   401p. (World's classics)
     Includes the short story: "The Bibulous
     Business of a Matter of Taste," (B5).

B68. Cuppy, William J., ed. <u>Murder</u> <u>without</u> <u>Tears</u>;
     <u>An</u> <u>Anthology</u> <u>of</u> <u>Crime</u>. New York: Sheridan
     House, 1946.   561p.
     Includes the short story: "In the Teeth of
     the Evidence," (B18).

B69. -----. <u>World's</u> <u>Greatest</u> <u>Mystery</u>
     <u>Stories</u>. Cleveland: World Pub. Co., 1943.
     299p.
     Includes the short story: "Suspicion," (B39).

B70. Daly, Maureen, ed. My Favorite Suspense
　　　　Stories. New York: Dodd, Mead, 1968.
　　　　275p.
　　　　Includes the short story: "The Inspiration
　　　of Mr. Budd," (B20).

B71. Detection Medley. London: Hutchinson, 1939.
　　　　528p.　New York: Dodd, Mead, 1940.　　528p.
　　　　Includes two short stories: "The Haunted
　　　Policeman," (B16), and "Striding Folly," (B38).
　　　This collection is edited by John Rhode, pseud.
　　　for Cecil John Charles Street.

B72. Dickinson, Susan, comp. The Case of the Vanishing
　　　　Spinster, and Other Mystery Stories. London:
　　　　Collins, 1972.　　256p.　(Illustrated)
　　　　Includes the short story: "The Inspiration
　　　of Mr. Budd," (B20). This work was illustrated
　　　by Robert Micklewright.

B73. Ellery Queen's Mystery Magazine. New York:
　　　　American Mercury, Inc., 1941+　　v.1+
　　　　Includes the following short stories:
　　　"The Man Who Knew How," Vol.2 (Winter, 1941),
　　　　　pp.103-114, (B24).
　　　"The Leopard Lady," Vol.4, No.1 (January, 1943),
　　　　　pp.111-127, (B22).

"The Vindictive Story of the Footsteps That Ran,"
Vol.6, No.25 (November, 1945), pp.75-87, (B44).

"The Poisoned Dow '08," Vol.11, No.51 (February,
1948), pp.38-46, (B32).

"The Necklace of Pearls," Vol.15, No.76 (March,
1950), pp.123-130, (B29).

"Suspicion," Vol.16, No.85 (December, 1950),
pp.83-95, (B39).

"The Haunted Policeman," Vol.19, No.102 (May,
1952), pp.17-33, (B16).

"Striding Folly," Vol.22, No.117 (August, 1953),
pp.99-109, (B38).

"Something Queer About Mirrors," i.e., "The Image
in the Mirror," Vol.43, No.9 (September,
1964), pp.67-87, (B17).

"The Power of Darkness," i.e., "The Incredible
Elopement of Lord Peter Wimsey," Vol.45,
No.5 (May, 1965), pp.46-66, (B19).

"The Queen's Square," Vol.49, No.4 (April, 1967),
pp.105-118, (B34).

"The Bibulous Business of a Matter of Taste,"
Vol.51, No.2 (February, 1968), pp.25-36, (B5).

B74. Ernst, John, ed. *Favorite Sleuths*. Garden City,
N.Y.: Doubleday, 1965.   322p.

Includes the short story: "The Adventurous
Exploit of the Cave of Ali Baba," (B3).

B75. Evans, Melvin, ed. *The Horizontal Reader; A Light
Tonic of Amusing Tales, Oddities, and
Irreverent Verse and Wisdom, Compounded for
Bedtime Use*. Garden City, N.Y.: Doubleday,
1961.   424p.

Includes the short story: "Suspicion," (B39).

B76. Fadiman, Clifton, ed. *Dionysus: a Case of Vintage
Tales About Wine*. New York: McGraw-Hill,
1962.   309p.

Includes the short story: "A Bibulous Business
of a Matter of Taste," (B5).

B77. -----. *The Joys of Wine*. With Sam
Aaron. New York: Abrams, 1975.   450p.

Includes the short story: "The Bibulous
Business of a Matter of Taste," on pages 408-417,
(B5).

B78. Ferguson, John DeLancey, ed. *Theme and Variation
in the Short Story*. New York: The Cordon Co.,
1938.   550p.

Includes the short story: "The Entertaining
Episode of the Article in Question," (B11).

B79. Fifty Famous Detectives of Fiction. London:
   Odhams Press, 1948. 696p. (Illustrated;
   Reprinted in 1951)
   According to: A Catalogue of Crime, (p.455),
  Miss Sayers was represented in this work.

B80. Grand Magazine. London: 1905-1940. 77 Volumes.
   According to James Sandoe, the short story:
  "The Man Who Knew How," is included in one of
  these volumes. No specific reference is given,
  but it probably appeared before 1933. See (B24)
  and (B45).

B81. Green, Roger Lancelyn, ed. Ten Tales of Detection....
   New York: Dutton, 1967. 204p.
   Includes the short story: "Absolutely
  Elsewhere," (B2).

B82. Harper's Bazaar. New York: Harper & Brothers,
   1868+ v.1+
   Vol.73 (February, 1938), pp.62-63, 130-135,
  includes the short story: "The Haunted Policeman,"
  (B16).

B83. Haycraft, Howard, ed. The Boy's Second Book of
   Great Detective Stories. New York: Berkeley
   Pub. Corp., 1964. 192p.
   Includes the short story: "The Adventurous
  Exploit of the Cave of Ali Baba," (B3).

B84. -----. <u>Fourteen</u> <u>Great</u> <u>Detective</u> <u>Stories</u>. New
York: Modern Library, 1949.   464p.
Includes the short story: "The Undignified
Melodrama of the Bone of Contention," (B41).

B85. -----. <u>Ten</u> <u>Great</u> <u>Mysteries</u>. With John Beecroft.
Garden City, N.Y.: Doubleday, 1959.   640p.
Includes the short story: "The Learned
Adventure of the Dragon's Head," (B21).

B86. -----. <u>Three</u> <u>Times</u> <u>Three</u>; <u>Mystery</u> <u>Omnibus</u>.
Garden City, N.Y.: Doubleday, 1964.
3 volumes in 1 (830p.)
Includes the short story: "In the Teeth of the
Evidence," (B18).

B87. -----. <u>A</u> <u>Treasury</u> <u>of</u> <u>Great</u> <u>Mysteries</u>. New York:
Simon & Schuster, 1957.   2v.
Includes the short story: "The Undignified
Melodrama of the Bone of Contention," in volume 2,
see (B41).

B88. Hitchcock, Alfred Joseph, ed. <u>Alfred</u> <u>Hitchcock</u>
<u>Presents</u> <u>Stories</u> <u>Not</u> <u>for</u> <u>the</u> <u>Nervous</u>. New
York: Random House, 1965.   363p.
Includes the short story: "The Abominable
History of the Man with   Copper Fingers," (B1).

B89. -----. <u>Alfred</u> <u>Hitchcock's</u> <u>Spellbinders</u> <u>in</u>
<u>Suspense</u>. Illustrated by Harold Isen.
New York: Random House, 1967.   206p.
Includes the short story: "The Man Who
Knew How," (B24).

B90. Kahn, Joan, ed. <u>The</u> <u>Edge</u> <u>of</u> <u>the</u> <u>Chair</u>, <u>Anthology</u>.
New York: Harper & Row, 1967.   560p.
Includes the short story: "Scrawns," (B35).

B91. Karloff, Boris, ed. <u>And</u> <u>the</u> <u>Darkness</u> <u>Falls</u>.
Cleveland and New York: World Pub. Co.,
1946.   631p.
Includes the short story: "The Cyprian Cat,"
(B8).

B92. Kimball, Rodney A., ed. <u>Short</u> <u>Story</u> <u>Reader</u>.
New York: The Odyssey Press, 1946.   460p.
Includes the short story: "Suspicion," (B39).

B93. Lee, Elizabeth, ed. <u>Murder</u> <u>Mixture</u>; <u>An</u> <u>Anthology</u>
<u>of</u> <u>Crime</u> <u>Stories</u>. London: Elek Books, 1963.
478p.
Includes the short story: "The Fountain
Plays," (B15).

B94. McGowan, Kenneth, ed. <u>Sleuths</u>; <u>Twenty-three</u>
<u>Great</u> <u>Detectives</u> <u>of</u> <u>Fiction</u> <u>and</u> <u>Their</u> <u>Best</u>
<u>Stories</u>. New York: Harcourt, Brace, 1931.   595p.

Includes the short story: "The Entertaining
Episode of the Article in Question," (B11).
This work also contains a valuable chronological
bibliography (pp.585-595).

B95. Manley, Seon, comp. <u>Grande</u> <u>Dames</u> <u>of</u> <u>Detection</u>;
<u>Two</u> <u>Centuries</u> <u>of</u> <u>Sleuthing</u> <u>by</u> <u>the</u> <u>Gentle</u> <u>Sex</u>.
Compiled with G. Lewis. New York: Lathrop,
Lee & Shepard, 1973.   224p.
Includes the short story: "The Learned
Adventure of the Dragon's Head," (B21).

B96. Margolies, Joseph A., ed. <u>Strange</u> <u>and</u> <u>Fantastic</u>
<u>Stories</u>; <u>Fifty</u> <u>Tales</u> <u>of</u> <u>Terror</u>, <u>Horror</u> <u>and</u>
<u>Fantasy</u>. New York; London: Whittlesey House,
McGraw-Hill, 1946.   762p.
Includes the short story: "The Cyprian
Cat," (B8).

B97. <u>My</u> <u>Best</u> <u>Detective</u> <u>Story</u>, <u>an</u> <u>Anthology</u> <u>of</u> <u>Stories</u>
<u>Chosen</u> <u>by</u> <u>Their</u> <u>Own</u> <u>Authors</u>. London: Faber &
Faber, 1931.   491p.
Includes the short story: "The Inspiration
of Mr. Budd," (B20).

B98. <u>My</u> <u>Best</u> <u>Thriller</u>, <u>an</u> <u>Anthology</u> <u>of</u> <u>Stories</u> <u>Chosen</u>
<u>by</u> <u>Their</u> <u>Own</u> <u>Authors</u>. London: Faber & Faber,
1933.   492p.
Includes the short story: "The Cyprian Cat," (B8).

B99. <u>Mystery</u> <u>League</u> <u>Magazine</u>. New York: Mystery
League, 1933+   v.1+

Vol.1, No.1 (October, 1933), pp.102-109,
contains the short story: "Suspicion," (B39).

B100. <u>Mystery</u>: <u>the</u> <u>Illustrated</u> <u>Detective</u> <u>Magazine</u>.
Chicago: Tower Magazines, Inc., 1929-1935.
12 volumes in 11.

Vol.9, No.1 (January, 1934), pp.19-21, 104,
106, and 108, includes the short story:
"Absolutely Elsewhere," (B2), under the title:
"Impossible Alibi."

B101. <u>Nash's</u> <u>Magazine</u>. London: 1909-1937+   v.1+

Included in the July, 1934, issue is the
short story: "The Milk-bottles," (B25). With
regard to this periodical, it was continued as
<u>Nash's</u> <u>and</u> <u>Pall</u> <u>Mall</u> <u>Magazine</u>, Oct. 1914 -
April 1927; continued as <u>Nash's</u> <u>Magazine</u>,
1927-1929; continued as <u>Nash's</u> <u>and</u> <u>Pall</u> <u>Mall</u>
<u>Magazine</u>, Oct. 1929 - Sept. 1937; and was
subsequently incorporated in <u>Good</u> <u>Housekeeping</u>.

B102. Postgate, Raymond William, ed. <u>Detective</u> <u>Stories</u>
<u>of</u> <u>Today</u>. London: Faber, 1940.   539p.

Includes the short story: "The Inspiration
of Mr. Budd," (B20).

B103. Queen, Ellery ₍pseud.₎ 101 Years' Entertainment,
the Great Detective Stories, 1841-1941.
New York: Modern Library, 1946, c1941.
995p.

Includes the short stories: "The Bibulous
Business of a Matter of Taste," (B5), and
"Suspicion," (B39).

B104. -----. Rogue's Gallery, the Great Criminals of
Modern Fiction. Boston: Little, Brown, 1945.
562p.

Includes the short story: "Blood Sacrifice,"
(B7).

B105. -----. Sporting Blood, the Great Sports Detective
Stories. Boston: Little, Brown, 1942.   360p.

Includes the short story: "The Learned
Adventure of the Dragon's Head," (B21). The
Introduction to this collection was written by
Grantland Rice.

B106. Richardson, Maurice, ed. Best Mystery Stories.
London: Faber, 1968.   224p.

Includes the short story: "The Adventurous
Exploit of the Cave of Ali Baba," (B3).

B107. Sandrus, Mary Y., ed. Famous Mysteries. Chicago:
Scott, Foresman, 1955.   298p.

Includes the short story: "Suspicion," (B39).

B108. <u>Senior Scholastic</u>. Teachers edition. Dayton,
Ohio: Scholastic Corp., 1936+   v,1+
Vol.31 (December 11, 1937), pp.3-5, includes
the short story: "The Stolen Stomach," i.e.,
"The Piscatorial Farce of the Stolen Stomach,"
(B31).

B109. Shibata, Tetsuo, ed. <u>The Confession and Two Other
Stories</u>. Tokyo: Kenkyusha, 1966.   114p.
Includes the short story: "The Inspiration
of Mr. Budd," (B20).

B110. <u>Six Against the Yard</u>. London: Selwyn & Blount,
1936.   288p.; Garden City, N.Y.:
Doubleday, Doran, 1936.   302p.; Garden
City, N.Y.: The Sun Dial Press, 1937.   302p.
The title of this collection varies somewhat,
and <u>Six Against Scotland Yard</u> is carried in
some editions. Has the sub-title: <u>In Which
Margery Allingham</u>, <u>Anthony Berkeley</u>, <u>Freeman Wills
Crofts</u>, <u>Father Ronald Knox</u>, <u>Dorothy L. Sayers</u>,
<u>and Russell Thorndike Commit the Crime of Murder</u>,
<u>Which Ex-Superintendent Cornish</u>,<u>C.I.D.</u>, <u>is
Called Upon to Solve</u>. Miss Sayers' "crime" is
her short story: "Blood Sacrifice," (B7), on
pages 207-242,   followed directly by Mr.
Cronish's comment, "They Wouldn't Believe Him!"

B111. Spectorsky, Auguste C., ed. <u>Man into Beast</u>;
       <u>Strange Tales of Transformation</u>. Garden
       City, N.Y.: Doubleday, 1947.   368p.
       Includes the short story: "The Cyprian
    Cat," (B8).

B112. <u>The Strand Magazine, an Illustrated Monthly</u>.
       London: G. Newnes, 1891+   v.1+
       Vol.94 (March, 1938), pp.482-494, includes
    the short story: "The Haunted Policeman," (B16).
    The cover has a brilliant color illustration
    of Lord Peter Wimsey dressed to the nines
    with top hat and white tie.

B113. Street, Cecil John Charles, ed. <u>Line-up</u>; <u>A</u>
       <u>Collection of Crime Stories by Famous</u>
       <u>Mystery Writers</u>. New York: Dodd, Mead,
       1940.   378p.
       Includes two short stories: "The Haunted
    Policeman," (B16), and "Striding Folly," (B38).

B114. Thomson, Henry D., ed. <u>The Mystery Book</u>.
       London: Odhams Press, 1934.   1079p.
       (Illustrated)
       Barzun in : <u>A Catalogue of Crime</u>, (pp.563-4),
    indicates that there is a contribution by
    Dorothy L. Sayers in this volume. (See H15).

B115. Wise, Herbert Alvin, ed. <u>Great</u> <u>Tales</u> <u>of</u> <u>Terror</u>
<u>and</u> <u>the</u> <u>Supernatural</u>. New York: Random
House, 1944.   1080p.

Includes the short story: "Suspicion," (B39).

B116. Wright, Lee, ed. <u>The</u> <u>Pocket</u> <u>Book</u> <u>of</u> <u>Great</u>
<u>Detectives</u>. New York: Pocket Books, 1941.

Barzun in: <u>A</u> <u>Catalogue</u> <u>of</u> <u>Crime</u>, (p.571),
indicates that Lord Peter Wimsey is included in
this collection. (See H15).

B117. -----. <u>Wicked</u> <u>Women</u>. New York: Pocket Books, 1960.

Barzun in: <u>A</u> <u>Catalogue</u> <u>of</u> <u>Crime</u>, (p.572),
indicates that there is a contribution by Dorothy
L. Sayers contained in this collection. (See H15).

Section C

<u>ESSAYS</u>

As a lecturer and essayist Dorothy L. Sayers talked and wrote about a wide range of subjects including theology, Dante, social problems, and literature. She possessed perhaps one of the most alert and interesting minds in England during her lifetime. Moreover, her style was so piquant that her writings would have charm even if her ideas were dull--which they were not. She was considered to be an unconventional thinker; however, her ideas were not conspicuously unpopular, even though she did delight in expressing them as pungently as possible.

In her religious essays, Miss Sayers' excellences of wit and style enable her to skate over what seems to be very thin theological ice at times. She had many interesting things to say and said them with a robust and cheerful common sense which is refreshing. With regard to her major interest, Miss Sayers set about building an earnest and convincing case for the

69

recognition of the importance of Dante's theology
and ethics as indispensible aids for the understanding
of his poetry.

Many of the essays cited in this section were
first prepared as lectures, addresses, or speeches.
Cross-references are given to the corresponding
essays, lectures, addresses, or speeches. Part I
lists each essay by title in alphabetical order with
a brief descriptive annotation. Part II lists book-
length essays; Part III, introductory essays; Part IV,
collections of essays; and Part V, anthologies or
periodicals containing essays. Each part is cross-
referenced for convenience in locating information
about each essay.

I. Individual Essays

C1. "...And Telling You a Story; a Note on the
Divine Comedy"

The author finds that instead of being
great, grim, religious, and intellectual, in
the Divine Comedy, Dante was, in reality, one
of the greatest story-tellers ever to set pen
to paper. This essay can be found in: Essays

Presented to Charles Williams (C119); and
Further Papers on Dante (C100).

C2. "Are Women Human?"

Originally this was an address given to
a Women's Society in 1938 (G1). Asked to explain
her views on feminism, the author summed up her
whole argument against aggressive feminism by
advocating individualism. This essay can be
found in: Are Women Human? (C97); and Unpopular
Opinions (C106).

C3. "Aristotle on Detective Fiction"

First given as a lecture (G2), the essay is
an amusing discussion of Aristotle's views in
The Poetics and how they relate to detective
fiction: the importance of the plot, the art
of false reasoning, and the difficulty of the
denouement. This essay can be found in: English;
the Magazine of the English Association (C117);
and Unpopular Opinions (C106).

C4. "The Art of Translating Dante"

Miss Sayers documents the various English
language translations of the Divine Comedy in
chronological order and discusses the ways in

which these translations differ. To this
discussion she adds her own evaluative comments.
This essay can be found in: <u>Nottingham</u> <u>Mediaeval</u>
<u>Studies</u> (C138).

C5. "The Beatrician Vision in Dante and Other Poets"

First delivered as a lecture (G3). The nature
and meaning of the Beatrician vision in poetry
are emphasized within a theological context.
This essay can be found in: <u>Nottingham</u> <u>Mediaeval</u>
<u>Studies</u> (C138), and <u>The</u> <u>Poetry</u> <u>of</u> <u>Search</u>... (C104).

C6. "Charles Williams: Poet's Critic"

First delivered as a conference lecture (G4).
Miss Sayers eulogizes the accomplishments of
her former teacher and Dante scholar. Apparently
Williams was not one to be taken lightly by the
literary world. This essay can be found in:
<u>Christian</u> <u>Letters</u>... (C98) under the title: "Dante
and Charles Williams," and <u>The</u> <u>Poetry</u> <u>of</u> <u>Search</u>...
(C104).

C7. "Christian Belief About Heaven and Hell"

An an Anglican theologian, Miss Sayers
gives a cogent and striking version of one
Christian view of the afterlife, including a

discussion of heaven and hell. This essay
can be found in: The Great Mystery of Life
Hereafter (C121), reprinted from the Sunday
Times (ca. Jan. 1957).

C8. "Christian Morality"

Sayers suggests that the Church has placed
too much emphasis on the regulation of bodily
appetites and the proper observance of holidays.
It has, in effect, made an alliance with Caesar
(the state) where money, not moral principles,
is the measure of value for society. This
essay can be found in: Christian Letters... (C98),
and Unpopular Opinions (C106).

C9. "The Church in War's Aftermath"

Miss Sayers examines the Church's role in
the "new age." The Church's duty with respect
to the new age will be "one and the same, namely
to bear resolute and incorruptible witness against
it." To survive the peace, however, the Church
must face new problems with realism. This essay
can be found in: Living Age (C133).

C10. "The Church's Responsibility"

First delivered as an address (G5). Miss

Sayers considers how Christian thought can be shaped to play a leading part in post-World War II reconstruction. She asserts that if the Church is to find its common soul it must contrive to root it in a common interest. This essay can be found in: <u>Malvern</u> <u>1941</u> (C135).

C11. "The City of Dis"

First delivered as a lecture (G6). The place and function of the heavenly community in the <u>Divine</u> <u>Comedy</u> are discussed in relation to projected reality. This essay can be found in: <u>Introductory</u> <u>Papers</u> <u>on</u> <u>Dante</u> (C102).

C12. "The Comedy of the <u>Comedy</u>"

First delivered as a lecture (G7). Is there really any comedy in the <u>Divine</u> <u>Comedy</u>? Sayers contends that one will find, if he or she looks for it, a comic attitude, a diffused spirit of high comedy permeating the whole poem and springing from two main sources: the characterization (particularly where Dante's own self portraiture is concerned) and the satiric intention. This essay can be found in: <u>Introductory</u> <u>Papers</u> <u>on</u> <u>Dante</u> (C102).

C13. "The Contempt of Learning in 20th Century
England"

A dialogue between Ego and Alter Ego of
why there seems to be a general contempt for
learning while practical knowledge goes begging
and standards of academic journalism are non-
existent. This essay can be found in: The
Fortnightly (C120).

C14. "The Cornice of Sloth"

Originally delivered as a lecture (G8).
The imagery and meaning of sloth in the Divine
Comedy are given a thorough examination in
light of modern scholarly interpretation. This
essay can be found in: Further Papers on Dante (C100).

C15. "Creative Mind"

First delivered as a lecture (G9). Words
to the scientist and the poet are not always
the same, points out Sayers. She seems to berate
the scientific community for not coming to grips
with the true meaning of words and their impact
upon the creative mind. This essay can be found
in: Christian Letters... (C98), and Unpopular
Opinions (C106).

C16. "Creed or Chaos?"

First delivered as a lecture (G10). Sayers contends that at the bottom of the religious war between Christendom and heathendom is a "violent and irreconcilable quarrel about the nature of God and the nature of man and the ultimate nature of the universe." She examines the nature of this war of dogma and what she thinks should be done about it. This essay can be found in: Christian Letters... (C98), and Creed or Chaos? (C99).

C17. "Dante and Milton"

Originally delivered as a lecture (G11). Sayers indicates that the surprisingly close parallelism between the careers of Milton and Dante makes a comparison easier and more fruitful than those between other pairs of writers whom critical convention habitually links together. This essay can be found in: Further Papers on Dante (C100).

C18. "Dante the Maker"

First delivered as a lecture (G12), this essay is a discourse on the structure of the Paradiso and the way Dante makes use of imagery to convey precise meaning. This essay can

be found in: <u>The Poetry of Search</u>... (C104).

C19. "Dante's Cosmos"

 Originally delivered as a lecture (G13).

Sayers discusses Dante's views of the cosmos

in light of history and the impact of science

on modern thought. The emphasis is on Dante's

smaller and more philosophical view. This essay

can be found in: <u>Further Papers on Dante</u> (C100).

C20. "Dante's Imagery: I. Symbolic"

 First delivered as a lecture (G14). Sayers

examines the symbolic imagery in the <u>Divine

Comedy</u> which involves the meaning and under-

standing Dante wished to convey. This essay

can be found in: <u>Introductory Papers on Dante</u>

(C102).

C21. "Dante's Imagery: II. Pictorial"

 Originally delivered as a lecture (G14).

The <u>Divine Comedy</u>, says Miss Sayers, is an

enchanting picture book where the vivid images

leap up to catch the eye. She demonstrates the

pictorial images that Dante used so well through-

out this classic work. This essay can be found

in: <u>Introductory Papers on Dante</u> (C102).

C22. "Dante's Virgil"

First delivered as a lecture (G15). In this essay Sayers deals with Virgil's symbolic significance in Dante's allegory and indicates how this symbolic significance dictates and is woven with the character and actions of Virgil as he appears in the first two books of the Divine Comedy. This essay can be found in: Further Papers on Dante (C100).

C23. "The Dates in The Red-Headed League"

This "spoof criticism" is a discussion of the chronological order of the dates in Conan Doyle's The Red-Headed League; also, a note on Dr. Watson's handwriting and forgeries of it. This essay can be found in: Christian Letters... (C98), The Colophon (C114), and Unpopular Opinions (C106).

C24. "Divine Comedy"

Sayers satirizes the different approaches to the life of Christ as revealed in a number of theatrical productions. She is not convinced that they make it either exciting or true-to-life. This essay can be found in: Unpopular Opinions (C106).

C25. "The Divine Poet and the Angelic Doctor"

First delivered as a lecture (G20). A far-reaching discourse on the influence of St. Thomas Aquinas on Dante, particularly with respect to method and historical orderliness. This essay can be found in: Further Papers on Dante (C100).

C26. "Dr. Watson, Widower"

Another of the Holmesian "spoof criticisms" dealing with the life of Watson after the death of his wife. This essay can be found in: Unpopular Opinions (C106).

C27. "Dr. Watson's Christian Name"

This "spoof criticism" pretty much settles the argument arising out of what was considered to be a printer's error, namely that of Dr. John H. Watson's middle name. It is a common assumption that Watson's Christian name is John, but his correct middle name has been disputed. Since his wife refers to him as James, Sayers contends that it is because the "H" in his signature does not stand for "Henry" (as was popularly assumed), but for "Hamish," the Scottish form of "James." This essay can be found in: Profile by Gaslight (C145), and Unpopular Opinions (C106).

C28. "The Dogma is the Drama"

      A serious but satirical essay in which Miss
Sayers attempts to clear up some misconceptions
of Christian orthodoxy by way of question and
answer dialogue. Example: "Q.: What does the
Church think of sex? A.: God made it necessary
to the machinery of the world, and tolerates it,
provided the parties (a) are married, and (b) get
no pleasure out of it." This essay can be found
in: <u>Christian Letters</u>... (C98), <u>Creed or Chaos?</u>
(C99), and <u>Strong Meat</u> (C105).

C29. "The Eighth Bolgia"

      First delivered as a lecture (G21). The
author discusses Canto XXVI of the <u>Inferno</u>
from a literary point of view to see how a major
poet, such as Dante, copes with the fundamental
task of telling a story in verse. This essay can
be found in: <u>Further Papers on Dante</u> (C100).

C30. "Emile Gaboriau, 1835 - 1873; the Detective Novelist's
        Dilemma"

      Although this essay was unsigned it is
undoubtedly Sayers' according to Sandoe. It is
a front-page story on the centenary of Gaboriau's

birth; also a biographical and critical tribute.
This essay can be found in: <u>Times</u> <u>Literary</u>
<u>Supplement</u> (C149).

C31. "The Enduring Significance of Dante"

Originally broadcast by the B.B.C., July 9,
1950. Miss Sayers discusses Dante's cosmology
and concludes that his view will last while
others will be cast aside. This essay can be
found in: <u>The</u> <u>Listener</u> (C131).

C32. "The English Language"

Sayers contends that the English language
is being polluted by the outside world and
that the English are not doing anything about
it. She offers many examples of this decadent
tendency. This essay can be found in: <u>Unpopular</u>
<u>Opinions</u> (C106). It is essentially the same as
"The King's English" (C47), with a minor omission.
Also given as a lecture (G22).

C33. "The Faust Legend and the Idea of the Devil"

First delivered as a lecture (G23). Miss
Sayers examines the role of the devil in
literature and compares this with his role
in the Faust legend. This essay can be found

in: <u>Christian Letters</u>... (C98), <u>The Poetry</u>
<u>of Search</u>... (C104), and <u>Publications of the</u>
<u>English Goethe Society: Papers</u>... (C118).

C34. "Fen Floods; Fiction and Fact"

Sayers discusses, somewhat autobiographically,
the Fenland floods as she knew them while growing
up in the Fen country, and how she used the
phenomenon as the ending to <u>The Nine Tailors</u>,
it being a parallel account of the Denver flood
of 1713. This essay can be found in: <u>The Spectator</u>
(C146).

C35. "Forgiveness"

"Forgiveness is a difficult matter, and no
man living is wholly innocent or wholly guilty,"
indicates the author. Sayers discusses the
various approaches to forgiveness as a Christian
principle and applies it to national understanding. This essay can be found in: <u>Unpopular</u>
<u>Opinions</u> (C106). Published first under a different
title; see (C36).

C36. "Forgiveness and the Enemy"

This essay is essentially the same as (C35),
published under the title: "Forgiveness." This
version of the essay first appeared in: <u>The</u>
<u>Fortnightly</u> (C120).

C37. "The Fourfold Interpretation of the <u>Comedy</u>"

The way for the soul to find God according to Dante is discussed by reference to four interpretations: historical, the moral sense, anagogical or mystical, and image. This essay can be found in: <u>Introductory Papers on Dante</u> (C102). It was undoubtedly delivered first as a lecture sometime during the early 1950's, but there is no indication of when.

C38. "Gaudy Night"

The title is the same as the author's novel. In this essay, Sayers gives a fascinating account of the creation of Lord Peter Wimsey, along with an explanation of the role of Harriet Vane. She concludes by saying that "the whole thing is a warning against inventing characters whose existence has to be prolonged through a long series of books. Et certes est-ce bien un grief labeur que d'excogiter cent contes drolatiques?" This essay can be found in: <u>The Art of the Mystery Story</u> (C124), and <u>Titles to Fame</u> (C140).

C39. "The Greatest Drama Ever Staged is the Official Creed of Christendom"

Sayers examines the life of Christ as a great

drama that develops the Christian creed. This essay can be found in: _Christian Letters_... (C98), _Creed or Chaos_? (C99), and _The Sunday Times_ (C147). The essay also appeared in a collection under a similar title; see (C101).

C40. "The Gulf Stream and the Channel"

The **peculiarities** of the British Isles and its people are examined in a highly satirical manner. The British, according to Sayers, do not have a climate, only weather, and they seem to relish their differentness. This essay can be found in: _Unpopular Opinions_ (C106).

C41. "Helen Simpson"

A tribute to Helen Simpson upon her death. Sayers had known her for about ten years, from the time that she (Simpson) had been elected as a member of the Detection Club. This essay can be found in: _The Fortnightly_ (C120).

C42. "Holmes' College Career"

The title of this "spoof criticism" is rather self-explanatory. Included is a chronology of Holmes' academic career, a bibliography, and a note on Reginald Musgrave. This essay can be found in: _Baker Street Studies_ (C110), and _Unpopular Opinions_ (C106).

C43. "How Free is the Press?"

Writing during the war, Sayers, while deploring the necessity of curtailing freedom of the press by government, does see some positive aspects about it. She discusses some abuses of this freedom by citing some personal examples. Stressed throughout are the responsibilities of a free press by its practitioners. This essay can be found in: Unpopular Opinions (C106).

C44. "The Human-Not-Quite-Human"

A decidedly feminist view of how women are considered to be not quite human in a world that is male oriented. Sayers admits, however, that at least one man (Christ) had the proper view of women. This essay can be found in: Are Women Human? (C97), and Unpopular Opinions (C106).

C45. "The Image of God"

A discussion of the nature of God, His physical features, and how the concepts of these have varied throughout history. This work was not intended as a separate essay, for it originally appeared as a chapter of: The Mind

<u>of</u> <u>the</u> <u>Maker</u> (C92). It can be found as an
essay in: <u>Christian</u> <u>Letters</u>... (C98).

C46. "Ink of Poppies"

Having received a letter appealing to women
to do something about the present state of the
world, Sayers is unmoved. Instead, she lashes
out in protest against the style of the letter
and its "hypnotic rumble of stupefying
polysyllables" which "we are accustomed to get
in political manifestos." This essay can be
found in: <u>The</u> <u>Spectator</u> (C146).

C47. "The King's English"

This is essentially the same essay as "The
English Language" (C32). It can also be found
in: <u>Nash's</u> <u>Magazine</u> (C136), and <u>Writing</u> <u>for</u> <u>the</u>
<u>Press</u> (C142).

C48. "Living to Work"

An essay originally written for broadcast
during wartime. It was cancelled because it
was supposedly too controversial. Generally,
Sayers discusses some principles of work,
expounding on two types: the kind which is a
hateful necessity and the other that is an
opportunity for enjoyment and self-fulfillment.
This essay can be found in: <u>Unpopular</u> <u>Opinions</u> (C106).

C49. "The Lost Tools of Learning"

First delivered as a lecture (G24). The
author discusses her highly controversial
views on the deficiencies of modern teaching
methods which fail to teach people how to
learn for themselves. This essay can be found
in: Education in a Free Society (C116), the
Hibbert Journal (C125), the National Review
(C137), and in The Poetry of Search... (C104).
Also published as a pamphlet (G68).

C50. "The Meaning of Heaven and Hell"

Probably first given as a lecture (G25).
The relationship between heaven and hell
receives considerable attention in Dante, the
understanding of which, Sayers contends, is
important to the vitality of Christianity.
This essay can be found in: Introductory Papers
on Dante (C102).

C51. "The Meaning of Purgatory"

Probably first given as a lecture (G26).
To Sayers, purgatory is not an eternal state
such as heaven or hell, but is a temporal
process continuous with, and of a quality
comparable to, our experience in this world. She

illuminates the special use of this concept
by Dante in the _Divine Comedy_. This essay can
be found in: _Introductory Papers on Dante_ (C102).

C52. "The Murder of Julia Wallace"

A brief treatment of a famous Liverpool
murder case. The case is perhaps the supreme
puzzle, made most appealing of all others by
the numerous circumstances, and Miss Sayers
treats it with all her genius for intellectual
and emotional understanding. This essay can be
found in: _The Anatomy of Murder_ (C108), _Great
Unsolved Crimes_ (C122), _Portable Murder Book_
(C127), and _Trial and Error_ (C128).

C53. "The Mysterious English"

Probably first delivered as a speech (G27).
Basically a political speech in which Miss
Sayers discusses the foundations of the British
political mind. She specifically points out how
others view the British as mysterious and how
they are generally complacent unless disturbed
by such things as internal strife or external
war. This essay can be found in: _Unpopular
Opinions_ (C106). Also published as a pamphlet
(G69).

C54. "Notes on the Way"

Miscellaneous reflections on war,
preparation for war, and money. Actually,
"Notes on the Way" is a weekly column for
distinguished guest writers to freely express
their views on any subject. This particular
column appeared in _Time_ _and_ _Tide_ (C148).

C55. "Oedipus Simplex: Freedom and Fate in Folk-lore
and Fiction"

Originally delivered as a speech (G28).
A Christian view of the Oedipus complex, or
simplex, as Sayers calls it. She deals at length
with the role of prophecy in folk-lore and
fiction. This essay can be found in: _Christian_
Letters... (C98), _The_ _Poetry_ _of_ _Search_... (C104),
and _Proceedings_ _of_ _the_ _Royal_ _Institution_ (C141).

C56. "On the Origin of Lord Peter Wimsey"

The author's reasons for creating this
famous fictional detective are given along
with some background information. This essay
can be found in: _The_ _Harcourt,_ _Brace_ _News_ (C123).

C57. "On Translating the _Divina_ _Commedia_"

First delivered as a lecture (G29). Sayers
admits that her translation aims at the common

reader. She discusses the problems involved
in her task along with her successes and
failures. This essay can be found in:
Nottingham Mediaeval Studies (C138), and
The Poetry of Search... (C104).

C58. "Other People's Great Detectives"

Sandoe indicates that this article, marking
the too-casual use of the word "great," suggests
tests for its application and glances at
Wilkie Collins' Sergeant Cuff, Chesterton's
Father Brown, E.C. Bentley's Philip Trent, and
a number of others. This essay can be found in:
Illustrated (C126).

C59. "The Other Six Deadly Sins"

First delivered as a lecture (G30). In
discussing society's overuse of the word
"immorality," Sayers wishes to remind us that
"lust" is not the only "deadly sin," and that
neither should it be confused with love nor
generally referred to as "immorality." This
essay can be found in: Christian Letters...
(C98), and Creed or Chaos? (C99). Also published
as a pamphlet (G70).

C60. "The Pantheon Papers"

This title is a collective one, given to a series of short satirical essays first appearing in _Punch_ (C139). In these essays Miss Sayers utilizes her dry and typical British wit and humor to poke fun at the materialism and other social ills in English society. These essays will appeal to those who are well acquainted with the _Book of Common Prayer_. Selections from these essays also appear in: _Christian Letters_... (C98).

C61. "The Paradoxes of the _Comedy_"

Possibly given as a lecture; however, there is no indication of when. Sayers states that paradoxes abound in Christian theology. Many of these confronted Dante and she examines the more prominent ones from the _Divine Comedy_. This essay can be found in: _Introductory Papers on Dante_ (C102).

C62. "Plain English"

The author's thoughts on "telegraphese;" in other words, the "ugly" English used in newspaper articles (a practice more in use before World War II than after). This essay can be found in: <u>Nash's</u> <u>Magazine</u> (C136), and <u>Unpopular</u> <u>Opinions</u> (C106).

C63. "Playwrights are not Evangelists"

Sayers indicates that Christian drama can be dangerous if not handled discretely. The playwright cannot, and should not, play the evangelist--"he cannot...compromise with his own convictions, ₍and₎ neither can he write his play with one ear cocked to hear what the Vatican is likely to say about it, and the other twisted round to discover how it is likely to go down at Geneva." This essay can be found in: <u>World</u> <u>Theatre</u> (C150).

C64. "Poetry, Language and Ambiguity"

First delivered as a lecture (G32). The author claims that poetry, history, and theology are alike in that they involve a philosophy of singleness because their chief concern is with unique events. This essay can be found in: <u>The</u> <u>Poetry</u> <u>of</u> <u>Search</u>... (C104).

C65. "The Poetry of Search and the Poetry of Statement"

First delivered as a lecture (G33). Sayers discusses two types of poetry: one that attempts to find out how one feels and the other that

tells what one knows. The former applies to
the present generation and the latter to an
earlier one. This essay can be found in: The
Poetry of Search... (C104).

C66. "The Poetry of the Image in Dante and Charles
        Williams"

        Originally given as an address (G34). A
comparison is made between the imagery used
by Dante and Charles Williams in their works
noting many similarities. This essay can be
found in: Further Papers on Dante (C100).

C67. "Pot versus Kettle"

        Sayers discusses her views on the efforts
of the Ministry of Information and the newspapers to cast aspersions on each other. This
discussion aroused some controversy. The essay
can be found in: Time and Tide (C148), along
with citations of answers and replies.

C68. "The Present Status of the Mystery Story"

        Sayers expresses her feeling that the
mystery story is becoming more and more
sophisticated in its appeal and is in danger of
losing the common touch. This essay can be
found in: London Mercury (C134).

C69. "Problem Picture"

A wide-ranging discussion of modern problems. Sayers applies her own experiences as an artist to the subject of the creative mind and its relationship to the common man. This work was not intended as an individual essay and appeared first as a chapter in: The Mind of the Maker (C92). It can be found as an essay in: Christian Letters... (C98).

C70. "The Psychology of Advertising"

Sayers concludes that we have the kind of advertising we deserve. The article apparently aroused some controversy and she replied to one of her critics in a letter under the same title as above. This essay and its reply can be found in: The Spectator (C146).

C71. "The Religions Behind the Nation"

The author comments on the support given to the nation in wartime. This essay can be found in: The Church Looks Ahead (C113).

C72. "A School of Detective Yarns Needed"

A brief article about writing detective stories and what the experts have done to improve the quality of their work. The article is unsigned but attributed to Sayers. This essay can be found in: _Literary Digest_ (C132).

C73. "Selections from the Pantheon Papers"

See "The Pantheon Papers," (C60).

C74. "A Sport of Noble Minds"

A brief version of her introduction to: _Great Short Stories of Detection, Mystery and Horror_, 1928, and _The Omnibus of Crime_, 1929. This essay can be found in: _Life and Letters Today_ (C130), and _Saturday Review of Literature_ (C143).

C75. "Strong Meat"

A religious examination of the purpose and experiences of the Christian as he or she faces the world and the ravages of time. This essay can be found in: _Christian Letters_... (C98), _Creed or Chaos?_ (C99), and _Strong Meat_ (C105).

C76. "The Teaching of Latin: A New Approach"

First delivered as a lecture (G36). A fascinating and amusing essay, chiefly auto-biographical, in which the author discusses her instruction in, not only Latin, but Greek, French, and German. This essay can be found in: _Latin Teaching: The Journal of the Association for the_

Reform of Latin Teaching (C129), and The
Poetry of Search... (C104).

C77. "The 'Terrible' Ode"

Sayers sets about the task of demolishing
a foolish piece of criticism. She refers to
the criticism that Dante, in his ode known as
the "Aspro parlar," is guilty of sadism or
sexual cruelty. She says that it is a poem
which says how much Dante suffers because a
girl will not have him for her lover, and how
much pleasure he could give to both of them if
she would. This essay can be found in: Nottingham
Mediaeval Studies (C138).

C78. "The Theologian and the Scientist; Dorothy L.
Sayers on Some Aspects of Fred Hoyle's
Recent Talks on 'The New Cosmology'"

Miss Sayers takes Mr. Hoyle to task for not
understanding Christians or the nature of
Christianity. This essay can be found in: The
Listener (C131).

C79. "They Tried to be Good"

Great Britain, the author concludes, is a
Christian nation that abhors war, but unwittingly
becomes involved no matter how good its intentions

are. She recounts the events that have brought her nation into the world's most terrible war and what state of public mind should exist for the remainder of it. This essay can be found in: Unpopular Opinions (C106).

C80. "Towards a Christian Aesthetic"

Sayers suggests, however tentatively, a method of establishing the principles of "Art Proper" upon that Trinitarian doctrine of the nature of the creative mind which, she thinks, really underlie it. She proceeds to state that on this foundation it might be possible to develop a Christian aesthetic which, finding its source and sanction in the theological center, would be at once more characteristically Christian and of more universal application than any aesthetic whose contact with Christianity is made only at the ethical circumference. This essay can be found in: Christian Letters... (C98), The New Orpheus (C144), Our Culture (C115), and Unpopular Opinions (C106).

C81. "The Translation of Verse"

First delivered as a lecture (G37). The problems that beset the translator of verse are examined in light of the author's experience. Some words of advice are also offered to those who would desire to do the same. This essay can be found in: The Poetry of Search... (C104).

C82. "Trials and Sorrows of a Mystery Writer"

Life is horribly real and ernest for the detective writer, says Miss Sayers, herself one of the most ingenious weavers of plots of mystery and crime. This essay can be found in: The Listener (C131).

C83. "The Triumph of Easter"

Miss Sayers examines the resurrection of Christ and the meaning of this singular event upon mankind. This essay can be found in: Creed or Chaos? (C99), and The Greatest Drama Ever Staged (C101). Reprinted from The Sunday Times, London (C147).

C84. "Vocation in Work"

Delivered originally as a speech (G38). Sayers urges at the close of World War II that there be a revolutionary change in attitude toward work. This essay can be found in: Bulletins from Britain (C111), and A Christian Basis for the Post-War World (C109).

C85. "A Vote of Thanks to Cyrus"

      The author claims to owe a great debt to Cyrus the Persian for the synthesis of history and the confutation of heresy which he provides in understanding the Bible. This essay can be found in: Christian Letters... (C98), and Unpopular Opinions (C106).

C86. "Vox Populi"

      This is basically a letter in essay form protesting the penalties administered under the "Silence Campaign" in Great Britain during the early part of the war. This essay can be found in: The Spectator (C146).

C87. "What Do We Believe?"

      A reaffirmation of Christian principles during wartime. The author discusses such themes as the belief in God, the creation of man in God's image, a belief in the Holy-Ghost and in Baptism. She apparently seeks a creative approach to Christian living. This essay can be found in: Christian Letters... (C98), and Unpopular Opinions (C106).

C88. "Why Work?"

      First delivered as an address (G39). More of

the author's ideas on the "right attitude"
toward work; delivered a year after her
first address on "Vocation in Work" (C84),
this address is on people's attitudes before,
during, and after the war. This essay can be
found in: Creed or Chaos? (C99).

C89. "Wimsey Papers; Being the War-Time Letters
and Documents of the Wimsey Family"

A weekly series of eleven installments,
chiefly letters, commenting upon the war from
the point of view of the Wimsey Family and
friends. It appears that Lord Peter is working
for the Foreign Office, "somewhere abroad,"
probably in Turkey. An announcement in the
January issue states that the articles will
no longer appear as a weekly series but at
"less regular intervals," although there were
apparently no further installments. This series
of essays can be found in: The Spectator (C146).

C90. "The Writing and Reading of Allegory"

First delivered as a lecture (G40). Allegory,
according to Sayers, is a distinct literary
form, whose aim and intent is to dramatize a
psychological experience so as to make it more

comprehensible. She claims that it is also show-
ing some resurgence to its former standing
in literature. This essay can be found in:
Christian Letters... (C98), and The Poetry
of Search (C104).

II. Book-Length Essays

C91. Begin Here: A War-Time Essay

>London: Gollancz, 1940.   160p.
>New York: Harcourt, Brace, 1941.   156p.
>   (Has the sub-title: A Statement of Faith)

"The author's purpose is to suggest how we
(Great Britain) may use the opportunity of the
war to think and plan creatively for the future
of our civilization."

C92. The Mind of the Maker

>London: Methuen, 1941.   186p.
>New York: Harcourt, Brace, 1941.   229p.
>New York: Meridian Books, 1956.   229p.
>Westport, Conn.: Greenwood Press, 1970.   229p.

An essay on Christian philosophy in which
the author attempts to explain the nature of
God, as Creator, by analogy with the creative
capacity of the human mind. She explains that
she is not writing as a Christian, but as a

professional writer, although she is not
disclaiming her belief in Christianity.

This is the first volume of the Bridgeheads
series, edited by Miss Sayers and Muriel St.
Clare Byrne. Two of the chapters: "Image of
God" (C45) and "Problem Picture" (C69), appear
as essays in the collection: <u>Christian Letters</u>...
(C98).

III. <u>Introductory Essays</u>

C93. "Biographical Note" (On Lord Peter Wimsey), by
his uncle Paul Austin Delagardie ₍i.e.,
Dorothy L. Sayers₎

In various places this title differs
slightly; see Sandoe (I9), p.79. This Note is
prefaced to reprints of <u>Whose Body</u>?, <u>Clouds of
Witness</u>, <u>Unnatural Death</u>, and <u>The Unpleasantness
at the Bellona Club</u> (London: Gollancz, 1935).
An announcement appeared in the <u>Times</u> ₍London₎
July 12, 1935, p.9e. The Note appeared in the
United States in 1938 in the combined edition
of <u>The Dawson Pedigree</u> and <u>Lord Peter Views the
Body</u> (New York: Harcourt, Brace, 1938).

At the beginning of most of her mysteries,

Sayers adds a note or some form of prefatory
statement that, in a sense, might be
considered as a mini-essay.

C94. "Introductions" to Great Short Stories of
Detection, Mystery and Horror. (1928,
1929, 1934) 3 vols. (Same in The Omnibus
of Crime which was published in the United
States)

"Here it should be noted," according to
Sandoe, that "these are among the most scholarly
and literate essays on the history, forms,
conventions, and status of the detective story."
The first essay was published in a shorter
version as "A Sport of Noble Minds," (C74).
This work also appeared in: Writing Detective
and Mystery Fiction (C112), The Art of the
Mystery Story (C124), and Detective Fiction:
Crime and Compromise (C107).

C95. "Introduction" to: The Moonstone, by Wilkie
Collins. London: J.M. Dent, 1944; New
York: E.P. Dutton, 1944. pp.v-xi.

Another of Miss Sayers' impeccable essays,
this one on Wilkie Collins' most popular novel,
and on his work as a detective fiction writer.

C96. "Introduction" to: <u>James I</u>., by Charles
Williams. London: Arthur Barker, 1951,
c1934; New York: Roy Publishers ₍n.d.₎.
pp.ix-xiii.

A tribute to Williams in which Miss
Sayers examines his style as a historical
writer--not his most notable area of scholarly
endeavor.

IV. <u>Collections of Essays</u>

C97. <u>Are Women Human</u>?
Grand Rapids, Mich.: Eerdmans, 1971.   47p.
The Introduction is by Mary McDermott Shideler.
Includes the essays: "Are Women Human?" (C2),
and "The Human-not-quite-Human" (C44). In these
essays Dorothy Sayers addresses herself to the
subject of women's rights and the role of women
in society. They can also be found in: <u>Unpopular
Opinions</u> (C106).

C98. <u>Christian Letters to a Post-Christian World</u>; <u>A
Selection of Essays</u>.
Grand Rapids, Mich.: Eerdmans, 1969.   236p.
This collection was selected and introduced

by Roderick Jellema. These essays reveal
Dorothy L. Sayers as a clear and sometimes
witty apologist for Christian creeds, as well
as a social and literary critic.

Contents:--Selections from the Pantheon
Papers, (C60).--The greatest drama ever staged,
(C39).--Strong meat, (C75).--The dogma is the
drama, (C28).--What do we believe? (C87).--
Creed or chaos? (C16).--A vote of thanks to
Cyrus, (C85).--The dates in The red-headed
league, (C23).--Towards a Christian aesthetic,
(C80).--Creative mind, (C15).--The image of God,
(C45).--Problem picture, (C69).--Christian
morality, (C8).--The other six deadly sins,
(C59).--Dante and Charles Williams, (C6).--The
writing and reading of allegory, (C90).--Oedipus
simplex, (C55).--The Faust legend and the idea
of the devil, (C33).

C99. Creed or Chaos? and Other Essays in Popular
Theology.

London: Methuen, 1947.   88p.
New York: Harcourt, Brace, 1949.   85p.

Seven personal essays dealing with such
religious beliefs as the doctrine of the

incarnation and the seven deadly sins. The
importance of dogma to religion is the general
theme running through these addresses which
have been previously published in pamphlet
form. They are considered provocative writings,
appealing to both clergy and laymen.

Contents:--The greatest drama ever staged,
(C39).--The triumph of Easter, (C83).--Strong
meat, (C75).--The dogma is the drama, (C28).--
Creed or chaos?, (C16).--Why work?, (C88).--
The other six deadly sins, (C59).

C100. Further Papers on Dante.

London: Methuen, 1957.   221p.
New York: Harper, 1957.   214p.

In this collection of essays and speeches,
Miss Sayers continues her lively discourses
on Dante which she began in the Introductory
Papers (C102) published in 1954. These papers
were not written for specialists but simply
for intelligent readers of Dante. They are by
no means superficial, but in the strict sense
they are not professional either. The attitude
she assumes in these lectures, despite her
obvious erudition, is that of the eager,

untutored reader who usually avoids the
ponderous classics because he wants to be
entertained, not instructed.

   Contents:--...And telling you a story, (C1).
--The divine poet and the angelic doctor, (C25).
--Dante's Virgil, (C22).--Dante's cosmos, (C19).
--The eighth bolgia, (C29).--The cornice of sloth,
(C14).--Dante and Milton, (C17).--The poetry of
the image in Dante and Charles Williams, (C66).

C101. The Greatest Drama Ever Staged.

   London: Hodder & Stoughton, 1938.   44p.

   A pamphlet on religious problems; it contains:
"The Greatest Drama Ever Staged," (C39), and
"The Triumph of Easter," (C83). Both were
reprinted from the Sunday Times, London (April,
1938).

C102. Introductory Papers on Dante.

   London: Methuen, 1954.   225p.
   New York: Harper, 1954.   225p.
   New York: Barnes & Noble, 1969.   225p.
      (Reprint of the 1954 edition)

   The preface to this work was written by
Barbara Reynolds. In this collection, Miss
Sayers addresses herself to the task of
interpreting the Christian message of Dante

for modern readers. In a series of papers
delivered to student audiences, she discusses
Dante's use of allegory, symbol, and imagery,
and explains the medieval assumptions so
unfamiliar to contemporary readers. Her central
objective, however, is to make the Catholic
doctrines of which Dante was the great poetic
expositor meaningful to modern men. This
companion to Dante studies makes The Divine
Comedy much less of a stumbling block to the
general reader.

Contents:--Dante's imagery, (C20; C21).--
The meaning of heaven and hell, (C50).--The
meaning of purgatory, (C51).--The four-fold
interpretation of the Comedy, (C37).--The city
of Dis, (C11).--The comedy of the Comedy, (C12).
--The paradoxes of the Comedy, (C61).

C103. A Matter of Eternity.Selections from the Writings
of Dorothy L. Sayers.

Oxford: A.R. Mowbray, 1973.   139p.
Grand Rapids, Mich.: Eerdmans, 1973.   139p.

Chosen and introduced by Rosamond Kent
Sprague. She offers a selection of quotable
passages from Miss Sayers' theological and
devotional writings on a number of themes,

including creation, sin, forgiveness, women,
and work. Within the various sections the
excerpts range in length from one sentence
to several pages; in content they represent
the full range of her work. Also included is
the first book appearance of the poem entitled
"For Timothy, in the Coinherence," (E21). The
only complete essay contained in this work is:
"The Lost Tools of Learning," on pages 107-135;
see (C49) for annotation.

C104. The Poetry of Search and the Poetry of Statement;
and Other Posthumous Essays on Literature,
Religion and Language.
London: Gollancz, 1963.   286p.

In this posthumous collection of twelve
occasional essays on related subjects, Miss
Sayers' talents as a scholar and translator of
Dante are fully displayed. Five of the essays
have to do with Dante in some way, exhibiting
not only considerable knowledge but great
sympathy for the author. Miss Sayers has some
pertinent remarks on the teaching of Latin, the
interest of which is increased by some autobio-
graphical reminiscence. The essays dealing more

strictly with literary criticism are not, perhaps, so original as the remainder of the book, but all she has to say is firmly and clearly stated. The layman will learn much about Dante from her, and readers in general will find this book as easy and pleasant in style as it is stimulating in content.

Contents:--The poetry of search and the poetry of statement, (C65).--Dante the maker, (C18).-- The Beatrician vision in Dante and other poets, (C5).--Charles Williams: poet's critic, (C6).-- On translating the Divina Commedia, (C57).-- The translation of verse, (C81).--The lost tools of learning, (C49).--The teaching of Latin: a new approach, (C76).--The writing and reading of allegory, (C90).--The Faust legend and the idea of the devil, (C33).--Oedipus simplex; freedom and fate in folk-lore and fiction, (C55). --Poetry, language and ambiguity, (C64).

C105. Strong Meat.

London: Hodder & Stoughton, 1939.   44p.

According to Miss Sayers, this was first published as a pamphlet. Published here in book form, the contents include: "Strong Meat," (C75),

and "The Dogma is the Drama," (C28). Both
of these essays are included in: Creed or
Chaos?, (C99).

C106. Unpopular Opinions.

> London: Gollancz, 1946.   190p.
> New York: Harcourt, Brace, 1947.   236p.

At her best, Dorothy L. Sayers wrote on
controversial subjects with a trenchancy which
recalls the early work of G.K. Chesterton. At
her worst, she scolded. The essays in this
collection are divided into three groups:
theological, political, and critical. In the
Introduction, Sayers indicated that the first
section courts unpopularity by founding itself
on theology and not on "religion." The second
will offend all those who use and enjoy
slatternly forms of speech, all manly men,
womenly women, and people who propose to
revive Christianity. In short, these essays
are distinctively individual commentaries on
Christian morality, religion, women, responsibility
of the press, and the use of the English language.
In addition, there is a group of studies on
Conan Doyle's Sherlock Holmes stories.

Contents:--Christian morality, (C8).--

Forgiveness, (C35).--What do we believe?
(C87).--Divine comedy, (C24).--A vote of thanks
to Cyrus, (C85).--Towards a Christian aesthetic,
(C80).--Creative mind, (C15).--The Gulf Stream
and the Channel, (C40).--The mysterious English,
(C53).--Plain English, (C62).--They tried to
be good, (C79).--Are women human? (C2).--
The human-not-quite-human, (C44).--Living to
work, (C48).--How free is the press? (C43).--
Holmes' college career, (C42).--Dr. Watson's
Christian name, (C27).--Dr. Watson, widower,
(C26).--The dates in The red-headed league,
(C23).--Aristotle on detective fiction, (C3).--
The English language, (C32).

V. Essays Appearing in Anthologies or Periodicals

C107. Allen, Richard Stanley, comp. Detective Fiction:
Crime and Compromise. Edited with David
Chacko. New York: Harcourt, Brace,
Jovanovich, 1974. 481p.

Includes the: "Introduction" to The Omnibus
of Crime, on pages 351-382. See (C94) for
annotation.

C108. The <u>Anatomy</u> <u>of</u> <u>Murder</u>; <u>Famous</u> <u>Crimes</u>
<u>Critically</u> <u>Considered</u> <u>by</u> <u>Members</u> <u>of</u> <u>the</u>
<u>Detection</u> <u>Club</u>. Edited by Helen Simpson.
London: John Lane, 1936.   335p.; New
York: Macmillan, 1937.   335p.
Includes the essay: "The Murder of Julia
Wallace," on pages 157-211. See (C52) for
annotation.

C109. Baker, Albert Edward, ed. <u>A</u> <u>Christian</u> <u>Basis</u>
<u>for</u> <u>the</u> <u>Post-War</u> <u>World</u>; <u>A</u> <u>Commentary</u> <u>on</u> <u>the</u>
<u>Ten</u> <u>Peace</u> <u>Points</u>. London: Student Christian
Movement Press, 1942.   120p.
Includes the essay: "Vocation in Work."
See (C84) for annotation.

C110. Bell, Harold Wilmerding, ed. <u>Baker-Street</u>
<u>Studies</u>. London: Constable, 1934.   223p.
Includes the essay:"Holmes' College Career,"
on pages 1-34. See (C42) for annotation.

C111. <u>Bulletins</u> <u>from</u> <u>Britain</u>. New York: British
Library of Information, 1940+   v.1+
Includes the essay: "Vocation in Work,"
No.103 (August 19, 1942), pp.7-10. See (C84)
for annotation.

C112. Burack, Abraham Saul, ed. <u>Writing</u> <u>Detective</u> <u>and</u>
<u>Mystery</u> <u>Fiction</u>. Boston: The Writer, Inc.,
1945.   237p.

Includes the introductory essay of: <u>Great</u>
<u>Short</u> <u>Stories</u> <u>of</u> <u>Detection</u>, <u>Mystery</u> <u>and</u> <u>Horror</u>,
which is the same in <u>The</u> <u>Omnibus</u> <u>of</u> <u>Crime</u>; in
the former, published under the title: "Detective
Fiction: Origins and Development," on pages 3-48.
See (C94) for annotation.

C113. <u>The</u> <u>Church</u> <u>Looks</u> <u>Ahead</u>; Broadcast Talks by
J.H. Oldham [and others] London: Faber &
Faber, 1941.   122p.

Includes the essay: "The Religions Behind
the Nation." See (C71) for annotation.

C114. <u>The</u> <u>Colophon</u>...; <u>A</u> <u>Quarterly</u> <u>for</u> <u>Booklovers</u>.
New York: Pynson [etc.] 1930+   v.1+

Includes the essay: "The Dates in <u>The</u> <u>Red-</u>
<u>Headed</u> <u>League</u>," Pt.17, No.10 (June, 1934),
[unpaged]. See (C23) for annotation.

C115. Demant, Vigo Auguste, ed. <u>Our</u> <u>Culture</u>: <u>Its</u>
<u>Christian</u> <u>Roots</u> <u>and</u> <u>Present</u> <u>Crisis</u>. London:
Society for Promoting Christian Knowledge,
1944.   113p. (Edward Alleyn Lectures,
1944)

Includes the essay: "Toward a Christian Aesthetic," See (C80) for annotation.

C116. Education in a Free Society. Anne Husted Burleigh, ed. Indianapolis: Liberty Fund, 1973.   182p.

Includes the essay: "The Lost Tools of Learning," on pages 145-167. See (C49) for annotation.

C117. English; The Magazine of the English Association. London: Published for the English Association by H. Milford, Oxford University Press, 1936+   v.1+

Includes the essay: "Aristotle on Detective Fiction," Vol.1, No.1 (1936), pp.23-35. See (C3) for annotation.

C118. English Goethe Society. Papers Read Before the Society. Cardiff, Wales [etc.]: 1923+   v.1+

Includes the essays: "The Faust Legend and the Idea of the Devil," (ns) Vol.15 (1946), pp.1-20. See (C33) for annotation.

C119. Essays Presented to Charles Williams. London: Oxford University Press, 1947.   145p.; Grand Rapids, Mich.: Eerdmans, 1966.   145p.;

Freeport, N.Y.: Books for Libraries,
1972, c1947.   145p.

Includes the essay: "...And Telling You
a Story: a Note on the <u>Divine</u> <u>Comedy</u>," on
pages 1-37. See (C1) for annotation.

C120. The <u>Fortnightly</u>. London: Chapman and Hall ⌈etc.⌉
1865+   v.1+

Includes the following essays: "The Contempt
of Learning in 20th Century England," Vol.153
(ns 147), (April 1940), pp.373-382; see (C13)
for annotation. "Forgiveness and the Enemy,"
Vol.155 (ns 149), (April, 1941), pp.379-383; see
(C35, C36) for annotation. "Helen Simpson,"
Vol.155 (January, 1941), pp.54-59; see (C41)
for annotation.

C121. The <u>Great</u> <u>Mystery</u> <u>of</u> <u>Life</u> <u>Hereafter</u>, by Dorothy
L. Sayers ⌈et al⌉ London: Hodder &
Stoughton, 1957.   126p.

Includes the essay: "Christian Belief
About Heaven and Hell." See (C7) for annotation.

C122. <u>Great</u> <u>Unsolved</u> <u>Crimes</u>, by Forty-two Contributors.
London: Hutchinson, 1935.   351p.

Includes the essay: "The Murder of Julia
Wallace," on pages 111-122. See (C52) for
annotation.

C123. The <u>Harcourt</u>, <u>Brace</u> <u>News</u>. New York: Harcourt, Brace,
      1936+   v.1+
      Includes the essay: "On the Origin of Lord
      Peter Wimsey," Vol.1 (July 15, 1936), pp.1-2.
      See (C56) for annotation.

C124. Haycraft, Howard, ed. <u>The</u> <u>Art</u> <u>of</u> <u>the</u> <u>Mystery</u>
      <u>Story</u>. New York: Simon & Schuster, 1946.
      545p.
      Includes the following essays: the Intro-
      duction to <u>The</u> <u>Omnibus</u> <u>of</u> <u>Crime</u>, on pages
      71-109, and entitled "The Omnibus of Crime
      (1928-29)"; see (C94) for annotation. Also,
      "Gaudy Night," on pages 208-221; see (C38)
      for annotation.

C125. The <u>Hibbert</u> <u>Journal</u>: <u>A</u> <u>Quarterly</u> <u>Review</u> <u>of</u>
      <u>Religion</u>, <u>Theology</u>, <u>and</u> <u>Philosophy</u>. London:
      Williams and Norgate [etc.] 1902+   v.1+
      Includes the essay: "The Lost Tools of
      Learning," Vol.46 (October, 1947), pp.1-13.
      See (C49) for annotation.

C126. <u>Illustrated</u>. London: Odhams Press, 1939+   v.1+
      Includes the essay: "Other People's Great
      Detectives," (April 29, 1939), pp.18-19. See
      (C58) for annotation.

C127. Jackson, Joseph Henry, ed. The Portable Murder
Book. New York: The Viking Press, 1945.
570p.

Includes the essay: "The Murder of Julia
Wallace." See (C52) for annotation.

C128. Kahn, Joan, comp. Trial and Terror. Boston:
Houghton, Mifflin, 1973.   569p.

Includes the essay: "The Murder of Julia
Wallace," on pages 103-153. See (C52) for
annotation.

C129. Latin Teaching: The Journal of the Association
for the Reform of Latin Teaching. London:
1919+   v.1+

Includes the essay: "The Teaching of Latin:
A New Approach," (October, 1952). The exact
volume and page numbers cannot be located
at the time of this writing. See (C76) for
annotation.

C130. Life and Letters To-Day. London: Brendin Pub.
Co., 1928+   v.1+

Includes the essay: "Sport of Noble Minds,"
Vol.4 (January, 1930), pp.41-54. See (C74) for
annotation.

C131. The Listener and B.B.C. Television Review.

        London: The British Broadcasting Corp.,

        1929+   v.1+

        Includes the following essays: "The Enduring

Significance of Dante," Vol.44 (July 20, 1950),

pp.87-89,(C31); "The Theologian and the

Scientist; Dorothy L. Sayers on Some Aspects

of Fred Hoyle's Recent Talks on 'The New

Cosmology,'" Vol.44 (November 9, 1950), pp.496-

497, 500, (C78); and "Trials and Sorrows of a

Mystery Writer," Vol.7 (January 6, 1932), p.26,

(C82).

C132. The Literary Digest. New York: Funk & Wagnalls,

        1890-1938.   125vols. in 128. (Title

        varies; merged into Time, May, 1938)

        Includes the essay: "A School of Detective

Yarns Needed," (September 23, 1922), p.33. See

(C72) for annotation.

C133. The Living Age. Boston: Littell & Son ₍etc.₎

        1844+   v.1+

        Includes the essay: "The Church in War's

Aftermath," Vol.360 (July, 1941), pp.441-445.

See (C9) for annotation.

C134. <u>The</u> <u>London</u> <u>Mercury</u>. London: The Field Press
ᵣetc.ᵧ 1919+   v.1+

Includes the essay: "The Present Status
of the Mystery Story," Vol.23 (November, 1930),
pp.47-52. See (C68) for annotation.

C135. Malvern Conference, Malvern College, Malvern,
Eng., 1941. <u>Malvern</u> <u>1941</u>: The Life of the
Church and the Order of Society Being the
Proceedings of the Archbishop of York's
Conference. London; New York ᵣetc.ᵧ:
Longmans, Green, 1941.   235p.

Includes the essay: "The Church's Responsibility,"
on pages 55-78. See (C10) for annotation. For
critical comment see <u>Time</u> (January 20, 1941),
pp.61-63, "For a New Society"; <u>The</u> <u>Sewanee</u>
<u>Review</u>, Vol.49 (July-September, 1941), pp.293-
302, "Piers Plowman Walks Again; A Note on the
Malvern Conference, by William Orton"; and a
review of the published proceedings in: <u>The</u>
<u>Spectator</u> (March 6, 1942), pp.237-238.

C136. <u>Nash's</u> <u>Magazine</u>. London: 1909-1937+   v.1+
(Title varies; see B101)

Includes the essays: "The King's English,"
(May, 1935; Coronation issue), pp.16-17, 88-90,

(C47); and "Plain English," (July, 1937),
pp.86-88, (C62).

C137. The National Review, a Weekly Journal of Opinion.
Orange, Conn.: National Weekly, 1955+   v.1+
Includes the essay: "The Lost Tools of
Learning," Vol.7 (August 1, 1959), pp.237-
244. See (C49) for annotation.

C138. Nottingham Mediaeval Studies. Cambridge [Eng.]:
Printed for the University of Nottingham
by W. Heffer, 1957+   v.1+ (annual)
Includes the following essays: "The Art
of Translating Dante," Vol.9 (1965), pp.15-31,
(C4); "The Beatrician Vision in Dante and Other
Poets," Vol.2 (1958), pp.3-23, (C5); "On
Translating the Divina Commedia," Vol.2 (1958),
pp.38-66, (C57); and "The 'Terrible' Ode,"
Vol.9 (1965), pp.42-54, (C77) for annotation.

C139. Punch. London: Published for the Proprietors
[etc.] 1841+   v.1+
Includes the following collection of short
essays known as "The Pantheon Papers": "The
Cosmic Synthesis," Vol.225 (November 2, 1953),
pp.16-19 (includes "Calendar of Unholy and Dead-
Letter Days"); "More Pantheon Papers," Vol.226

(January 6, 1954), p.60, and (January 13, 1954),
p.84; "The Polar Synthesis: A Sermon for
Cacophony-Tide (Reprinted from the Schisminster
Perish Magazine," Vol.226 (January 20, 1954),
p.124. Illustrations by Norman Mansbridge.
See (C60) for annotation.

C140. Roberts, Denys Kilham, ed. Titles to Fame.
London; New York: T. Nelson, 1937.   242p.
Includes the essay: "Gaudy Night," on pages
73-95. See (C38) for annotation.

C141. Royal Institution of Great Britain, London.
Notices of the Proceedings at the Meetings
of the Members..., with Abstracts of the
Discourses Delivered.... London: Printed
by W. Clowes, 1851+   v.1+
Includes the essay: "Oedipus Simplex: Freedom
and Fate in Folklore and Fiction," Vol.36 (1955),
pp.162+   See (C55) for annotation.

C142. Russell, Leonard. Writing for the Press. London:
A. & C. Black, 1935.   150p.; New York:
Macmillan, 1935.   150p.
Includes the essay: "The King's English,"
on pages 88-104. See (C47) for annotation.

C143. The Saturday Review of Literature. New York:
  Time, Inc. [etc.] 1924+   v.1+
  Includes the essay: "A Sport of Noble
Minds," Vol.6 (August 3, 1929), pp.22-23.
See (C74) for annotation.

C144. Scott, Nathan A., ed. The New Orpheus: Essays
  Toward a Christian Poetic. New York:
  Sheed & Ward, 1964.   431p.
  Includes the essay: "Towards a Christian
Aesthetic," on pages 3-20. See (C80) for
annotation.

C145. Smith, Edgar Wadsworth, ed. Profile by Gaslight;
  An Irregular Reader about the Private Life
  of Sherlock Holmes. New York: Simon and
  Schuster, 1944.   312p.
  Includes the essay: "Dr. Watson's Christian
Name," on pages 180-186. See (C27) for annotation.

C146. The Spectator. A Weekly Review of Politics,
  Literature, Theology, and Art. London:
  F.C. Westley [etc.]   1828+   v.1+
  Includes the following essays: "Fen Floods:
Fiction and Fact," Vol.158 (April 2, 1937),
pp.611-612, (C34); "Ink of Poppies," Vol.158
(May 14, 1937), pp.897-898, (C46); "The Psychology

of Advertising," Vol.159 (November 19, 1937),
pp.896-898, (C70); the reply to criticism of
the essay is located in Vol.159 (December 10,
1937), p.1056; "Vox Populi," Vol.165 (August 2,
1940), p.117, (C86); "The Wimsey Papers,"
Vol.163, pp.672-674, 736-737, 770-771, 809-810,
859-860, 894-895, 925-926 -- Vol.164, pp.8-9,
38-39, 70-71, 104-105 (November 17, 1939 -
January 26, 1940), see (C89) for annotation.

C147. The Sunday Times. London: 1822+   no.1+
          (Newspaper)

       Includes the following essays: "The Greatest
Drama Ever Staged," (April, 1938); see (C39)
for annotation. "The Triumph of Easter,"
(April, 1938); see (C83) for annotation.
The essay "Christian Belief about Heaven and
Hell" also appeared here (ca. January, 1957);
see (C7) for annotation.

C148. Time and Tide. London: Time and Tide Pub. Co.,
          192?+   v.1+

       Includes the following essays: "Notes on
the Way," Vol.21 (June 15, 1940), pp.633-634;
continued,   (June 22, 1940), pp.657-658, (C54);
"Pot versus Kettle," Vol.21 (August 10, 1940),

pp.826-828; answered: Vol.21 (August 24, 1940), p.863, in a letter from Mr. Tom Harrisson; reply from Miss Sayers in Vol.21 (August 31, 1940), p.884; from Mr. Harrisson in Vol.21 (September 7, 1940), p.906; see (C67) for annotation.

C149. <u>Times</u>, London. <u>Literary Supplement</u>. London:
1902+   v.1+

Includes the essay: "Emile Gaboriau, 1835-1873; the Detective Novelist's Dilemma," (November 2, 1935), pp.677-678. See (C30) for annotation.

C150. <u>World Theatre</u>. ₍Bruxelles, etc., Elsevier, etc.₎
1950+   v.1+

Includes the essay: "Playwrights are not Evangelists," Vol.5 (1955-56), pp.61-66. See (C63) for annotation.

Section D

<u>DRAMATIC</u> <u>WORKS</u>

There are some writers who have achieved success
in an area remote from playwriting and yet have displayed
a dramatic flair which has surprised no one more than
themselves. Dorothy L. Sayers was most certainly an
example, for she had been associated with the field
of detective fiction where her careful confections
concerning Lord Peter Wimsey had and still are relished
by many. Her first venture into the drama was a
pleasant, if rather mild, melodrama, <u>Busman's</u> <u>Honeymoon</u>
(1936), in which she portrayed her favorite hero
with the collaborative efforts of Muriel St. Clare
Byrne. A year later she revealed her true interest
in the stage in her composition of <u>The</u> <u>Zeal</u> <u>of</u> <u>Thy</u>
<u>House</u> (1937), a poetic and religious drama written
for production at Canterbury. This was high quality,
with a sensitiveness of expression and dramatic sweep.
The same may be said of <u>The</u> <u>Devil</u> <u>to</u> <u>Pay</u> (1939), which
causes Miss Sayers to be classed with the younger
poetic dramatists. She also wrote for radio drama-
tization, her most notable work being <u>The</u> <u>Man</u> <u>Born</u>

126

to Be King (1941), a play-cycle based on the life
of Christ and presented on the B.B.C.

In this section, where a play or broadcast
has been published, the publication information
is provided immediately under the title. Where
appropriate, explanatory information is given
regarding the play and additional sources.

I. Plays

D1. Busman's Honeymoon; A Play in Three Acts.
          New York: The Dramatists Play Service,
              1939.   144p. (Diagram)
          Written in collaboration with Muriel St.
     Clare Byrne. English publication of the dramatic
     version of this work preceded its appearance
     in novel form; see (A1). The play was produced
     at the Comedy Theatre in London on December 16,
     1936, with Dennis Arundell in the lead. See
     reviews in the Times (December 17, 1936), p.14b;
     and the Illustrated London News, Vol.189
     (December 26, 1936), p.1200, and Vol.190
     (January 2, 1937), p.27 (photos). It had an
     American tryout during the week of July 12-17,

1937, at the Westchester Playhouse, Lawrence
Farms, Mt. Kisco, New York; the production was
given brief notice in The New York Times
(July 13, 1937), p.3. Included in the
published version of the play are an Author's
Note and a Note to Publishers (being detailed
instructions on how to safely set up the murder
weapon: a hanging cactus pot). There are only
a few minor differences between the play and
the novel, the novel being basically an expanded
version of the play. This play is also contained
in: Famous Plays of 1937 (D15).

D2. Christ's Emperor.

Performed at St. Thomas's Church, Regent
Street, February 5-26, 1952. This play is a
shortened version of The Emperor Constantine (D4).
Although Sayers was always actively involved in
the productions of her plays, this marked the
first time where she was actually named as
director, along with Graham Suter. Reported in
the Times (January 11, 1952), p.6e.

D3. The Devil to Pay.

        Canterbury: H.J. Goulden, Ltd., 1939.   63p.
        London: Gollancz, 1939.   112p.
        New York: Harcourt, Brace, 1939.   147p.
          (Illustrated)
        Reprinted in Four Sacred Plays. London:
          Gollancz, 1948. (D5).

First produced at Canterbury in the Chapter
House during the Canterbury Festival, June
10-17, 1939, under the management of the Friends
of the Cathedral. Directed by Harcourt Williams.
Later performed in London.

This poetic drama retells "the famous history
of John Faustus the Conjuror of Wittenberg in
Germany; how he sold his immortal soul to the
Enemy of Mankind, and was served XXIV years
by Mephistopheles, and obtained Helen of Troy
to his paramour, with many other marvels; and
how God dealt with him at last." (Sub-title).

In this play Miss Sayers combines an interest
in theological argument with a nice command
of English prose and poetry. The blank verse
passages will, of course, not challenge
comparison with Marlowe, but they will stand
beside most English dramatic poetry; they have
the right copiousness of image and pulse of
rhythm and must be very agreeable matter for
an actor used to the clipped, monosyllabic
stuff of ordinary stage dialogue.

D4. The Emperor Constantine: A Chronicle.

> London: Gollancz, 1951.   191p.
> New York: Harper Brothers, 1951.   191p.

Performed at the Playhouse Theatre, Colchester, July 3, 1951. This work is an ambitious religious chronicle play covering the years from 305 A.D. to 326 A.D., when Christianity became the official religion of the Roman Empire which suppressed the Arian heresy at the Council of Nicaea and moved its head-quarters to Constantinople. Action zigzags over the entire Roman Empire, the list of characters is enormous, the structure episodic, and the machinery of pageantry sometimes overwhelms the story line. Those interested in the early history of the Chruch will find it rewarding while others may find all the theological hair-splitting a tiring experience.

D5. Four Sacred Plays.

> London: Gollancz, 1948.   352p.

This collection of four previously published plays that Dorothy L. Sayers wrote and intro-duced includes: The Zeal of Thy House (D9),

The <u>Devil</u> <u>to</u> <u>Pay</u> (D3), <u>He</u> <u>That</u> <u>Should</u> <u>Come</u>
(D12), and <u>The</u> <u>Just</u> <u>Vengeance</u> (D6).

D6. <u>The</u> <u>Just</u> <u>Vengeance</u>.

> London: Gollancz, 1946.   80p.
> Reprinted in:<u>Four</u> <u>Sacred</u> <u>Plays</u>,
>   pp.275-352, (D5).

The Lichfield Festival Play for 1946, Lichfield Cathedral, June 15, 1946. This very
serious modern miracle play of "Man's
insufficiency and God's redemptive act, set
against the background of contemporary crisis,"
was presented at the 750th anniversary festival
of Lichfield Cathedral. After the performance,
Miss Sayers, Frank Napier the producer, and
Anthony Hopkins the composer, were presented
to the Queen.

D7. <u>Love</u> <u>All</u>.

A light farce which appeared at the Torch
Theatre, London, in April, 1940. It apparently
was not received too well by the critics,
although the audiences seemed to enjoy it. No
bibliographical record can be located proving
publication of this play. Reviews can be found
in: <u>Times</u> ₍London₎ (April 10, 1940), p.6e; <u>New</u>
<u>Statesman</u> <u>and</u> <u>Nation</u>, Vol.19 (April 13, 1940),

p.493; and _Time_ _and_ _Tide_, Vol.21 (April 13, 1940), p.392, along with a sketch of the plot.

D8. The _Mocking_ _of_ _Christ_.

> In: _Catholic_ _Tales_ _and_ _Christian_ _Songs_.
> Oxford: Blackwell, 1918. pp.43-53.

This work forms Miss Sayers' first attempt at a miracle play, although obviously it was never intended for acting. Written in verse, the play portrays Christ just prior to the crucifixion. See Weales' _Religion_ _in_ _Modern_ _English_ _Drama_, pp.165-166, (H48).

D9. The _Zeal_ _of_ _Thy_ _House_.

> London: Gollancz, 1937.   110p.
> New York: Harcourt, Brace, 1937.   110p.
> Reprinted in: _Four_ _Sacred_ _Plays_, pp.7-103,
> (D5).

First played at Canterbury for the Canterbury Festival, June 12-18, 1937. Presented by the Friends of Canterbury Cathedral, and produced by Harcourt Williams and Frank Napier, with Mr. Williams playing William of Sens. It was presented in London on March 29, 1938, at the Westminster Theatre, and later played on a provincial tour. It was because of this tour, and the money needed to finance it, that Miss

Sayers consented to use Lord Peter Wimsey
in an advertisement, much to the dismay of
his fans; see the letter, "Whither Wimsey?"
(G61).

The play itself is the story of the foreign
architect William of Sens, brought to England
to reconstruct the choir at Canterbury after its
destruction by fire in 1174. This play was
included in: Religious Drama (D17), and Famous
Plays of 1938-39 (D16).

II. Broadcasts

D10. "'Behind the Screen' - III," The Listener,
       Vol.4 (July 2, 1930), pp.28-30.
       Broadcast by the B.B.C. on June 28, 1930.
A mystery serial, with Hugh Walpole on June 14,
1930; Agatha Christie on June 21; Anthony
Berkeley on July 5; E.C. Bentley on July 12;
and Father Ronald Knox on July 19. These
broadcasts were apparently done by the authors
on Saturday nights at 9:20 p.m.

D11. The Golden Cockerel.
       A play based upon the fairy tale by Pushkin;

broadcast by the B.B.C. on December 27, 1941.
Announced in: The Bookseller, No.1876
(November 20, 1941), p.457; and The Listener
(December 18, 1941), p.834.

D12. He That Should Come; A Nativity Play in One Act.

London: Gollancz, 1936.   80p.
Reprinted in: Four Sacred Plays, (D5).

"First performed in the original broadcast
version on the London national transmission
(B.B.C.) and from Broadcasting House, on
Christmas Day, 1936." This play, according to
Miss Sayers, was "to show the birth of Christ
against its crowded social and historical
background."

D13. The Man Born to Be King: A Play-Cycle on the
Life of Our Lord and Saviour Jesus Christ.

London: Gollancz, 1943.   343p.
New York: Harper, 1943.   339p.

This work was written specifically for
broadcasting. It was presented by the B.B.C.,
December 1941 - October 1942; produced by Val
Gielgud. Actually, this is a sequence of 12 plays
based on the life of Christ and later published
with the addition of the author's preface and
lengthy notes on the intent and characterizations

of each play. It is reverent and, on the
whole, orthodox, although the author
anticipates that some of her dramatic
expedients and scriptural interpretations
may be criticized by the literal-minded. Miss
Sayers' recognition of the likeness between
the Roman-Jewish situation of 2000 years ago
and Anglo-Indian colonial relations during the
late 40's and early 50's, contributes toward
a very effective reconstruction of the gospel
narrative. The series on the B.B.C. caused
some controversy at first, but those who
objected to the project were soon overruled
by the Central Religious Advisory Committee
to the B.B.C. and the Board of Governors who
saw no harm in broadcasting the series. Reported
in the Times (January 9, 1942), p.2d; and
(January 10, 1942), p.2e 4*. The series has
been re-broadcast many times since, and as
recently as January - March, 1975. A discussion
can be found in G.C. Weales' Religion in Modern
English Drama, pp.170-175, (H48).

Contents:--Dedicatory: The Makers.--
Foreword, by Dr. J.W. Welch.--Author's Introduction.--

Production Note by Val Gielgud.--<u>The</u> <u>Man</u>
<u>Born</u> <u>to</u> <u>Be</u> <u>King</u>:--(1) Kings in Judea.--
(2) The King's herald.--(3) A certain nobleman.
--(4) The heirs to the kingdom.--(5) The bread
of heaven.--(6) The feast of tabernacles.--
(7) The light and the life.--(8) Royal progress.
--(9) The King's supper.--(10) The princes of
this world.--(11) King of sorrows.--(12) The
King comes into His own.

    The U.S. edition lacks Dr. Welch's Foreword
and Val Gielgud's Production Note.

D14. "'The Scoop' - I," <u>The</u> <u>Listener</u>, Vol.5 (January
       14, 1931), pp.70-71.

    Broadcast on the B.B.C., January 10, 1931
(Part 1) through April 4, 1931 (Part 12), with
each episode written and read by the authors:
Miss Sayers on January 10, 1931; Agatha Christie
on January 17; E.C. Bentley on January 24;
Agatha Christie on January 31; Anthony Berkeley
on February 14; Freeman Wills Crofts on February
21; Clemence Dane on February 28; Mr. Bentley on
March 7; Mr. Berkeley on March 14; Miss Dane
on March 21; Freeman Wills Crofts on March 28;
and Miss Sayers on April 4: "'The Scoop' - XII, The

Final Scoop," The Listener, Vol.5 (April 8,
1931), pp.600-601.

III. Anthologies of Plays

D15. Famous Plays of 1937....

London: Gollancz, 1937.   775p.

Includes the play: Busman's Honeymoon on
pages 285-428, (D1).

D16. Famous Plays of 1938-1939.

London: Gollancz, 1939.   661p.

Includes the play: The Zeal of Thy House
on pages 9-93, (D9).

D17. Religious Drama.

New York: Meridian Books, 1957+   v.1+

This series is selected and introduced by
Marvin Halverson. Includes the play: The Zeal
of Thy House, Vol.1, pp.267-339. See (D9) for
annotation.

Section E

<u>POETRY</u>

Since Dorothy L. Sayers was so involved with
the Italian poet Dante, it seems only natural that
she would be greatly interested in poetry as a form
of literary expression. In fact, her first major
published work was a collection of poems, <u>Op</u>. <u>I</u>.,
published in 1916. Although she is not generally
known for her poetic prowess, she was able to achieve
an appealing religious lyric of good quality. Most
of her poetry seems to be on religious subjects,
although she did some on war-time topics as well as
short stanzas appended to some of her other works.

The poems in Part I are listed in alphabetical
order followed by a very brief annotation. Part II
lists collections, and Part III, anthologies and
periodicals containing her poetry. Like the other
sections of this work, all of the poems cited are
cross-referenced to their sources.

I. Individual Poems

E1. "Aerial Reconaissance"

A lengthy poem on war and the destruction it causes. This poem can be found in: The Fortnightly (E58).

E2. "Alma Mater"

A long verse featuring Helen of Troy as heroine. This poem can be found in: Op. I. (E55).

E3. "Byzantine"

Recounts the unchangeableness of Christ. This poem can be found in: Catholic Tales (E54).

E4. "Carol"

A song in verse to the new-born Christ. This poem can be found in: Catholic Tales (E54).

E5. "Carol for Oxford"

A poetic song extolling the virtues of Oxford. This poem can be found in: Catholic Tales (E54).

E6. "The Carpenter's Son"

A poem about the desires of the carpenter's son. This poem can be found in: Catholic Tales (E54).

E7. "Christ ·the Companion"

Lines related to the companionship of Christ for everyday living. This poem can be found in: Catholic Tales (E54).

E8. "Christus Dionysus"

Three stanzas on the god of wine at the gate. This poem can be found in: Catholic Tales (E54).

E9. "The Dead Man"

A verse apparently about the difference between good and evil. This poem can be found in: Catholic Tales (E54).

E10. "Dead Pan"

Seven stanzas on the death of Christ. This poem can be found in: Catholic Tales (E54).

E11. "Desdichado"

Lines on the earthly mission of Christ. This poem can be found in: Catholic Tales (E54).

E12. "The Drunkard"

A poem of seven stanzas relating to the reality of Christ. This poem can be found in: Catholic Tales (E54).

E13. "The Elder Knight"

A verse on the wisdom of age and the learning

of youth. This poem can be found in: <u>Op</u>. <u>I</u>.
(E55).

E14. "The English War"

Patriotic verses following a statement
made by Philip Jordan in a broadcast. This
poem can be found in: <u>Times Literary Supplement</u>
(E69).

E15. "Epiphany Hymn"

A song in verse on the gift of the Magi.
This poem can be found in: <u>Catholic Tales</u> (E54).

E16. "Epitaph for a Young Musician"

Lines on God smiting England in her dalliance.
This poem can be found in: <u>Op</u>. <u>I</u>. (E55), and
<u>Oxford Magazine</u> (E64).

E17. "Fair Erembours; A Song of the Web. French, XII C."

A translation of a 12th century French poem.
This poem can be found in: <u>Oxford Poetry, 1917</u>
(E66).

E18. "Fair Shepherd"

A poem on Christ as the good shepherd and
how the sheep will not heed him. This poem
can be found in: <u>Catholic Tales</u> (E54).

E19. "For Albert, Late King of the Belgians"

A rather bitter poem of four stanzas. This

poem can be found in: <u>Life</u> <u>and</u> <u>Letters</u> <u>Today</u>
(E62).

E20. "For Phaon"

Verses on the everlasting quality of poets
and poetry. This poem can be found in: <u>Oxford</u>
<u>Poetry, 1919</u> (E68).

E21. "For Timothy, in the Coinherence"

This poem was written around October 24, 1948,
upon the death of Timothy White, a cat belonging
to Muriel St. Clare Byrne. In March 1973, she
read it aloud on a radio program, and it was
subsequently published in: <u>The</u> <u>Listener</u> (E62a);
and <u>A</u> <u>Matter</u> <u>of</u> <u>Eternity</u>, pp. 138-139, (C103).

E22. "The Gates of Paradise"

A lengthy verse on Judas Iscariot. This poem
can be found in: <u>Op</u>. <u>I</u>. (E55).

E23. "The House of the Soul: Lay"

A narrative poem on the torments of the
soul. This poem can be found in: <u>Catholic</u> <u>Tales</u>
(E54).

E24. "Hymn in Contemplation of Sudden Death"

A song in verse about being prepared for
death at any time. This poem can be found in:
<u>Op</u>. <u>I</u>. (E55), and <u>Oxford</u> <u>Magazine</u> (E64).

E25. "I Will Build Up My House From the Stark
Foundations"

A poem in two stanzas, placed at the
beginning of the author's collection of verse:
Op. I. (E55).

E26. "Justus Judex"

A poem dealing with the role of Christ in
judgement. This poem can be found in: Catholic
Tales (E54).

E27. "The Last Castle"

A series of verses apparently celebrating
the close of an Oxford life. Includes the
shorter titles: "War-time," "Pipes," "Carol,"
"Reckoning," "Womanliness," "Harvest," "Snap-
dragons," "Self-defense," and "Symbol." This
poem can be found in: Op. I. (E55).

E28. "Last Morning in Oxford"

A reflective thought on college life. This
poem can be found in: Op. I. (E55).

E29. "Lay"

A rather lengthy narrative poem about
Oxford, prefaced by a quotation (in French)
from Eustache Deschamps' L'Art de Dictier. This
poem can be found in: Op. I. (E55), and Oxford
Poetry, 1915 (E65).

E30. "Lignum Vitae"

A short verse on the healing of nations.
This poem can be found in: <u>Catholic</u> <u>Tales</u> (E54).

E31. "Lord, I Thank Thee--"

An anti-war poem. It can be found in:
<u>London</u> <u>Calling</u> (E61), and <u>Britain</u> (E57). It
was also privately published (Stamford, Conn.:
The Overbrook Press, 1943. 8p. 100 copies).

E32. "A Man Greatly Gifted"

A light and descriptive poem about the
dusk of June. This poem can be found in:
<u>Op</u>. <u>I</u>. (E55).

E33. "A Matter of Brittany"

A poem in praise of Brittany. This poem can
be found in: <u>Op</u>. <u>I</u>. (E55), and <u>The</u> <u>Fritillary</u> (E59).

E34. "The Mocking of Christ: A Mystery"

This poem, actually a miracle play,
portrays Christ just prior to the crucifixion.
This poem can be found in: <u>Catholic</u> <u>Tales</u> (E54).

E35. "Obsequies for Music"

A sort of secular oratorio. This poem can be
found in: <u>The</u> <u>London</u> <u>Mercury</u> (E63).

E36. "ΠΑΝΤΑΣ ΕΑΚΥΣΩ"

A poem about the rebellion of the soul
against Christ, and how it is inevitable that
one must ultimately come to love Him. This
poem can be found in: Catholic Tales (E54).
A weak, non-academic translation of the title
is: "Relieve the Wounds."

E37. "The Poem"

A personal reflection. This poem can be
found in: The London Mercury (E63).

E38. "Pygmalion"

Fourteen stanzas on Pygmalion. This poem
can be found in: Oxford Poetry, 1918 (E67).

E39. "Rex Doloris"

A poem on the burden of Christ. This poem
can be found in: Catholic Tales (E54).

E40. "Rondels"

A rondel-type poem essentially about Oxford.
It includes the shorter verses entitled: "Going-
down Play," and "To M.J." This poem can be
found in Op. I. (E55).

E41. "Sacrament"

Lines on Christ and the sacrament. This poem
can be found in: Catholic Tales (E54).

E42. "Sion Wall"

A poem about the crucifixion. This poem can be found in: <u>Catholic</u> <u>Tales</u> (E54).

E43. "A Song of Paradise"

A song in verse about the pleasures of paradise. This poem can be found in: <u>Catholic</u> <u>Tales</u> (E54).

E44. "Sympathy"

Twenty-two lines on "the web that we call truth." This poem can be found in: <u>Oxford</u> <u>Poetry</u>, <u>1919</u> (E68).

E45. "Target Area"

A poem addresses to Fraulein Felsmer of Frankfurt, who was formerly Miss Sayers' piano teacher. This poem can be found in: <u>The</u> <u>Fortnightly</u> (E58), and <u>The</u> <u>Atlantic</u> <u>Monthly</u> (E56).

E46. "There is no Remedy for This"

A verse about Oxford, placed opposite the Table of Contents in: <u>Op</u>. <u>I</u>. (E55).

E47. "The Three Kings"

Three stanzas on the Magi and their gifts to Christ. This poem can be found in: <u>Op</u>. <u>I</u>. (E55).

E48. "To the Interpreter, Harcourt Williams"

Lines prefixed to <u>The</u> <u>Devil</u> <u>to</u> <u>Pay</u>, p.3, (D3).

E49. "The Triumph of Christ"

A short poem on the Resurrection. This poem can be found in: <u>Catholic</u> <u>Tales</u> (E54).

E50. "Vials Full of Odours"

A love poem in three stanzas. This poem can be found in: <u>Oxford</u> <u>Poetry</u>, <u>1919</u> (E68).

E51. "War Cat"

A lengthy poem concerning a cat, and others trying to survive during the Second World War in Britain. This poem can be found in: <u>The</u> <u>Poet's</u> <u>Cat</u> (E60), and <u>Time</u> <u>and</u> <u>Tide</u> (E68a).

E52. "White Magic"

A five-stanza poem apparently relating to the miracles of Christ. This poem can be found in: <u>Catholic</u> <u>Tales</u> (E54).

E53. "The Wizard's Pupil"

A four-stanza poem apparently on the teaching of Christ. This poem can be found in: <u>Catholic</u> <u>Tales</u> (E54).

II. Collections of Poetry

E54. Catholic Tales and Christian Songs.

>Oxford: Blackwell, 1918.   63p.
>New York: McBride, 1918.   63p.

Louis Untermeyer says that "it is no pretty abstraction, but a warm and altogether human godhead that animates these poems. Miss Sayers is especially successful when she adopts Mediaeval concepts and archaic forms; 'The house of the soul' is a brilliant technical example of the sometimes monotonous lay; the carols are quaint and individual; even the attempted canonization of a few nursery rhymes skims safely over the thin ice of burlesque. And 'The mocking of Christ,' half-masque, half mystery play, is a startling blend of history, picture making and irony."

Contents:--Desdichado (E11).--The triumph of Christ (E49).--Christ the companion (E7).-- The wizard's pupil (E53).--The dead man (E9).-- The carpenter's son (E6).--The drunkard (E12).-- Justus judex (E26).--White magic (E52).--Lignum vitae (E30).--Christus Dionysus (E8).--Dead Pan (E10).--Rex doloris (E39).--Sacrament (E41).--

Sion wall (E42).--Byzantine (E3).--Epiphany
hymn (E15).--Carol (E4).--Fair shepherd (E18).
--A song of paradise (E43).--Carol for Oxford
(E5).--The mocking of Christ: a mystery (E34).--
The house of the soul: lay (E23). Includes
also the poem with the Greek title (E36).

E55. Op. I.

> Oxford: Blackwell, 1916.   71p.
> New York: Longman, Green, 1916.   71p.
>   (Adventurers All, a series of young poets
>   unknown to fame, No.9)

This collection of poetry was Dorothy L.
Sayers' first published book. While these
poems are not always understandable with respect
to their meaning, they do show a fluency of
style that was to be a Sayers trademark throughout her life.

Contents:--I will build up my house from the
stark foundations (E25).--There is no remedy for
this (E46).--Alma mater (E2).--Lay (E29).--
The last castle (E27).--The gates of paradise
(E22).--The three kings (E47).--Matter of
Brittany (E33).--A man greatly gifted (E32).--The
elder knight (E13).--Hymn in contemplation of
sudden death (E24).--Epitaph for a young musician
(E16).--Rondels (E40).--Last morning at Oxford(E28).

III. Anthologies and Periodicals Containing Poems

E56. The Atlantic Monthly, a Magazine of Literature,
　　　　Science, Art, and Politics. Boston: Phillips,
　　　　Sampson [etc.] 1857+　　v.1+
　　　Includes the poem: "Target Area," Vol.173
　　(March, 1944), pp.48-50. See (E45) for
　　annotation.

E57. Britain. New York: British Information Service,
　　　　1942+　　v.1+
　　　Includes the poem: "Lord, I Thank Thee,"
　　Vol.1 (November, 1942), pp.37-41. See (E31) for
　　annotation.

E58. The Fortnightly.　London: Chapman and Hall [etc.]
　　　　1865+　　v.1+
　　　Includes the following poems: "Aerial
　　Reconaissance," Vol.160 (ns 154), (October, 1943),
　　pp.268-270, (E1); "Target Area," Vol.161 (ns, no. 927)
　　(March, 1944), pp.181-184, see (E45) for annotation.

E59. The Fritillary, Magazine of the Oxford Women's
　　　　Colleges. Oxford: 1923+　　v.1+
　　　Includes the poem: "Matter of Brittany,"
　　(E33). The author mentions this source in a note
　　in Op. I., p.8, but no specific reference is given.

E60. Gooden, Mona, comp. The Poet's Cat; An
Anthology. London, Toronto: G.G. Harrap,
1946.   115p.
Includes the poem: "War Cat," on pages
95-98. See (E51) for annotation.

E61. Jameson, Storm. London Calling. New York, London:
Harper, 1942.   322p.
Includes the poem:"Lord, I Thank Thee,"
on pages 293-298. See (E31) for annotation.

E62. Life and Letters Today. London: Brendin Pub. Co.,
1928+   v.1+
Includes the poem: "For Albert, Late King
of the Belgians," Vol.26 (July, 1940), p.36.
See (E19) for annotation.

E62a. The Listener and B.B.C. Television Review.
London: The British Broadcasting Corp.,
1929+   v.1+
Includes the poem: "For Timothy, in the
Coinherence," Vol.89 (March 15, 1973), p.337.
See (E21) for annotation.

E63. The London Mercury. London: The Field Press ₍etc.₎
1919+   v.1+
Includes the following poems: "Obsequies
for Music," Vol.3 (January, 1921), pp.249-253,(E35);

"The Poem," Vol.4 (October, 1921), p.577, see
(E37) for annotation.

E64. The Oxford Magazine: or, University Museum....
London: Printed for the authors, 1768+   v.1+
Includes the following poems: "Hymn in
Contemplation of Sudden Death," see (E24); and
"Epitaph for a Young Musician," see (E16). The
author's note on page 8 of Op. I. indicated
that the above poems are included in the
Oxford Magazine but no specific reference is
given.

E65. Oxford Poetry, 1915. Edited by G.D.H. Cole and
Thomas Wade Earp. Oxford: Blackwell, 1915.
71p.
Includes the poem: "Lay," on pages 50-57.
See (E29) for annotation.

E66. Oxford Poetry, 1917. Edited by Wilfred R. Childe,
Thomas W. Earp, and Dorothy L. Sayers.
Oxford: Blackwell, 1918.   60p.
Includes the poem: "Fair Erembours; A Song
of the Web. French XII C." on pages 52-53. See
(E17) for annotation.

E67. Oxford Poetry, 1918. Edited by Thomas W. Earp,
E.F.A. Geach, and Dorothy L. Sayers. Oxford:

Blackwell, 1919.   56p.

Includes the poem: "Pygmalion," on
pages 46-48. See (E38) for annotation.

E68. Oxford Poetry, 1919. Edited by Thomas W. Earp,
Dorothy L. Sayers, and Siegfried Sassoon.
Oxford: Blackwell, 1920.   62p.

Includes the following poems: "For Phaon,"
on page 50, see (E20); "Sympathy," on page 51,
(E44); and "Vials Full of Odours," on page 52,
see (E50) for annotation.

E68a. Time and Tide. London: Time and Tide Pub. Co.,
192?+   v.1+

Includes the poem: "War Cat," Vol.24
(December 4, 1943), p.994. See (E51) for annotation.

E69. Times, London. Literary Supplement. London:
1902+   v.1+

Includes the poem: "The English War,"
(September 7, 1940), p.445. See (E14) for
annotation.

TRANSLATIONS

Dorothy L. Sayers achieved in her fictional
works many melodramatic but gripping situations.
Many of her admirers were disappointed when, from
the late 1930's onward, she dropped the writing of
detective fiction partly for religious drama and
partly for popular Christian apologetics. She was,
perhaps, not so effective as she imagined in either
of these fields, but she had begun her literary
career as a poet and as a student of medieval French
literature. In the final decade of her life, her
main energies were concentrated on translating and
expounding Dante, having in mind that wide new audience
for serious writing which is "literate" rather than
"educated." For that task, into which she invested
much energy, time, good will, and ingenuity, she
deserves permanent gratitude.

This section is arranged chronologically with
appropriate information about each translation.

F1. Thomas, Anglo-Norman poet, 12th cent. _Tristan
    in Brittany, Being the Fragments of the
    Romance of Tristan Written in the XII
    Century by Thomas the Anglo-Norman._

    London: Ernest Benn, 1929.   220p.
    New York: Payson & Clarke, 1929.   220p.

    The brief prose sketch connecting the
various fragments of the poem is condensed
from Joseph Bédier's summary in his edition
of the poem published 1902-05. Nothing quite
takes the place of the story in its medieval
form, but this version is spirited and smooth.
Here is the famous description of London, one
whose twenty lines fit the city quite as well
today as in the Middle Ages, and here are all
the tricks and defiances by which the famous
love affair had its way. The fitted fragments
are in alternating prose and verse, and the
delightful introduction is by George Saintsbury.

F2. Dante Alighieri. _The Heart of Stone_, Being the
    Four Canzoni of the "Pietra" Group, done
    into English by Dorothy L. Sayers.

    Witham, Essex: J.H. Clarke, 1946.   16p.
        (Illustrated)

    Has a cover title with "Christmas 1946"

added. The wood engravings were done by Norah
Lambourne.

F3. Dante Alighieri. _The Comedy of Dante Alighieri,
the Florentine_.

> Harmondsworth, Middlesex: Penguin Books,
>   1949-63.   3v. (Illustrated)
> Baltimore, Md.: Penguin Books, 1950-63.
>   3v. (Illustrated)
> New York: Basic Books, 1962.   3v.
>   (Illustrated with a selection of William
>   Blake's drawings)

A translation of the _Divina Commedia_ in
terza rima: Cantica I, _Hell_ (1949); Cantica II,
Purgatory (1955); Cantica III, _Paradise_ (1962).
Of _Paradise_, Sayers completed twenty cantos,
and fragments of the remaining thirteen, before
her death in 1957. It was her wish that Dr.
Barbara Reynolds complete the translation,
which she did in 1962. Sayers wrote introductions
to the first two cantiche: _Hell_ (May 1948,
pp.9-66), and _Purgatory_ (September 1954, pp.9-71);
she also appended copious notes.

Although there is some disagreement among
scholars, it is generally agreed that Sayers'
colloquial translation is a good one, and that
she succeeds, where others have not, in
capturing Dante's humor. Gilbert Cunningham points
out that Sayers "must be given credit, together

with her publishers, for having made Dante a
commercial proposition, and no doubt her
translation in many cases provided an insight
into the <u>Divine</u> <u>Comedy</u>." See Gilbert Cunningham's
<u>The</u> <u>Divine</u> <u>Comedy</u> <u>in</u> <u>English</u>, (H20); and <u>The</u>
<u>Literatures</u> <u>of</u> <u>the</u> <u>World</u> <u>in</u> <u>English</u> <u>Translation</u>:
<u>A</u> <u>Bibliography</u>; <u>The</u> <u>Romance</u> <u>Languages</u>, Vol.3,
pt.1, p.58.

F4. Chanson de Roland. <u>The</u> <u>Song</u> <u>of</u> <u>Roland</u>.

Harmondsworth ₍Eng.₎: Penguin Books, 1957.
206p. (Illustrated)
Baltimore, Md.: Penguin Books, 1957.   206p.
(Illustrated)

Translated from the French; begun when Miss
Sayers was an undergraduate at Oxford, and
completed some forty years later. The Introduction is an historical background of the work
(pp.7-44).

Section G

MISCELLANEOUS WORKS

There are several categories of items produced
by Dorothy L. Sayers that are related to some of the
previous sections but are a little more diverse in
nature. These are collected in this section under
appropriate subject headings with cross-references
to other related sections.

I. Addresses, Lectures, Speeches

G1. Are Women Human?
A speech delivered at a women's society
in 1938. Also published as an essay (C2; C97).

G2. Aristotle and Detective Fiction
A lecture delivered at Oxford, March 5,
1935. Later delivered at Conway Hall, London,
before the English Association, June 21, 1935.
Reported in the Times (June 24, 1935), p.12c.
Also published as an essay; see (C3).

158

G3. The Beatrician Vision in Dante and Other Poets

Delivered as the Herford Memorial Lecture
to the Manchester Dante Society, March 14, 1956.
Also published as an essay (C5).

G4. Charles Williams: Poet's Critic

A lecture delivered to a conference held at
Milland Place, Liphook, Hants., August 23, 1955.
Also published as an essay (C6).

G5. The Church's Responsibility

A lecture delivered at Malvern, January 8,
1941. Also published as an essay (C10).

G6. The City of Dis

A lecture delivered to the Confraternitas
Historica, Sidney Sussex College, Cambridge
[n.d.] Also published as an essay (C11).

G7. The Comedy of the Comedy

A lecture delivered at the Summer School of
Italian Studies at Magdalen College, Oxford,
August 16, 1949. Also published as an essay
(C12).

G8. The Cornice of Sloth

A lecture delivered at the Summer School of
Italian Studies in 1950. Also published as an
essay (C14).

G9. <u>Creative</u> <u>Mind</u>

A lecture delivered to the Humanities Club
of Reading, February, 1942. Also published as
an essay (C15).

G10. <u>Creed</u> <u>or</u> <u>Chaos</u>?

A lecture delivered at the Biennial Festival
of the Church Tutorial Classes Association,
Derby, May 4, 1940. Also published as an essay
(C16).

G11. <u>Dante</u> <u>and</u> <u>Milton</u>

A lecture delivered to the Summer School
of Italian Studies in 1952. Also published as
an essay (C17).

G12. <u>Dante</u> <u>the</u> <u>Maker</u>

A lecture delivered to the Cambridge University
Italian Society, May 8, 1956, under the title
<u>Dante</u> <u>Faber</u>: <u>Structure</u> <u>in</u> <u>the</u> <u>Poetry</u> <u>of</u> <u>Statement</u>.
Also published as an essay (C18).

G13. <u>Dante's</u> <u>Cosmos</u>

A lecture delivered at the Royal Institution
of Great Britain in 1951. Also published as an
essay (C19).

G14. <u>Dante's</u> <u>Imagery</u>: I. <u>Symbolic</u>; II. <u>Pictorial</u>

Two lectures delivered to the Summer School

of the Society for Italian Studies in 1947.
Also published as essays:(C20) and (C21).

G15. Dante's Virgil

A lecture delivered to the Virgil Society
in 1948. Also published as an essay (C22).

G16. Detective Novelists

A lecture delivered at a dinner of the
University Section and the Authors' and
Journalists' Section of the Forum Club. Reported
in the Times (November 27, 1930), p.5d.

Sayers explains that it takes great
effort and hard work to write detective stories,
and, therefore, more sympathy should be felt
for the agonies they endure.

G17. The Detective Story

An address delivered at the Czechoslovak
Institute, January, 1942. Reported in the Times
Literary Supplement (January 31, 1942), p.49,
and in the New York Times (March 3, 1942), p.21.

A general discussion with comments on the
necessity for the enjoyment of detective novels,
the danger of introducing too much human
psychology, and the Englishman's view of
detection as a "good hunt,... a sport very
much in the English manner."

G18. <u>Detective</u> <u>Stories</u> <u>as</u> <u>a</u> <u>Token</u> <u>of</u> <u>Virtue</u>

A lecture delivered as chief guest
of the Stationers' and Newspaper Makers'
Company luncheon, Stationers Hall, February
15, 1939. Reported in the <u>Times</u> (February 16,
1939), p.11f.

Miss Sayers claims that the reading and
writing of detective fiction are highly
moral occupations.

G19. <u>The</u> <u>Dictatorship</u> <u>of</u> <u>Words</u>

A lecture delivered as President of the
Modern Language Association and on freedom
of the press and the vicious contemporary
misuse of words, Reported in the <u>Times</u>
(January 6, 1939), p.7a.

G20. <u>The</u> <u>Divine</u> <u>Poet</u> <u>and</u> <u>the</u> <u>Angelic</u> <u>Doctor</u>

A lecture delivered to the Aquinas Society,
1946. Also published as an essay (C25).

G21. <u>The</u> <u>Eighth</u> <u>Bolgia</u>

A lecture delivered at a Summer School
of Italian, Jesus College, Cambridge, August,
1946, Also published as an essay (C29).

G22. <u>English</u> <u>Language</u>

A lecture delivered at the annual luncheon

of the English Association, London, July 3,
1948. Reported in the _Times_ (July 5, 1948),
p.6d. Also published as an essay, (C32).

G23. The _Faust_ _Legend_ _and_ _the_ _Idea_ _of_ _the_ _Devil_

A lecture delivered to the English Goethe
Society, February 22, 1945. Also published as
an essay, (C33).

G24. The _Lost_ _Tools_ _of_ _Learning_

A lecture delivered at a Vacation Course
in Education, Oxford, 1947. Also published
as an essay, (C49), and in pamphlet form, (G68).

G25. The _Meaning_ _of_ _Heaven_ _and_ _Hell_

A lecture delivered to the Summer School
of the Society for Italian Studies in 1948.
Also published as an essay, (C50).

G26. The _Meaning_ _of_ _Purgatory_

A lecture delivered at the Summer School
of the Society for Italian Studies in 1948.
Also published as an essay,(C51).

G27. The _Mysterious_ _English_

A speech delivered in London in 1940.
Also published as an essay, (C53), and in
pamphlet form, (G69).

G28. Oedipus Simplex: Freedom and Fate in Folk-lore
and Fiction

A lecture delivered to the Royal Institution
of Great Britain, November 11, 1955. Also published
as an essay,(C55).

G29. On Translating the Divina Commedia

A lecture delivered at a course for Italian
teachers of English, organized by the British
Council at Girton College, Cambridge, August,
1954. Also published as an essay, (C57).

G30. The Other Six Deadly Sins

A lecture delivered to the Public Morality
Council, Westminster, October 23, 1941. Also
published as an essay, (C59), and in pamphlet
form, (G70).

G31. Our National Attitude Toward the Theatre

A lecture delivered during the Canterbury
Festival, at the Chapter House. Reported in
the Times (June 16, 1939), p.12b.

Miss Sayers compares the English attitude
toward theatres and churches: it would be a
shame to lose them for they are pleasant
enough; so someone should take steps--(not
ourselves, however).

G32. Poetry, Language and Ambiguity

A lecture delivered to the Oxford
University Socratic Scoiety, June 3, 1954.
Also published as an essay, (C64).

G33. The Poetry of Search and the Poetry of Statement

A lecture delivered to the Oxford University
Spectator Club, on October 30, 1956. Also
published as an essay, (C65).

G34. The Poetry of the Image in Dante and Charles
Williams

An address delivered to the Chelmsford
Arts Association in 1952. Also published as
an essay, (C66).

G35. Religious Drama and Production

A lecture to be delivered at the joint
meeting of the Coventry Diocesan Youth Council
and the Friends of Coventry, September 30, 1939,
at Coventry Cathedral. Announced in the Times
(August 1, 1939), p.15e.

G36. The Teaching of Latin: A New Approach

A lecture delivered to the Association for
the Reform of Latin Teaching, August 26, 1952.
Also published as an essay, (C76).

G37. The Translation of Verse

A lecture delivered to the Oxford
University English Club, March 6, 1957.
Also published as an essay, (C81).

G38. Vocation in Work

A speech delivered at Brighton, March 1941.
Also published as an essay, (C84).

G39. Why Work?

An address delivered at Eastbourne,
April 23, 1942. Also published as an essay,
(C88).

G40. The Writing and Reading of Allegory

Delivered as the second Sarah Walker
Memorial Lecture, at the Training College,
Darlington, November 10, 1954. Also published
as an essay, (C90).

II. Bibliography

G41. "William Wilkie Collins (1824-1889)," in
The Cambridge Bibliography of English
Literature, Frederick Wilse Bateson, ed.
New York: Macmillan; Cambridge [Eng.]: The
University Press, 1941-1957.   5v.
This bibliography is located in Vol.3, on

pages 480-482, and was contributed by Miss
Sayers. The last item listed in the bibliography,
under "Biography and Criticism," is "Sayers,
D.L. Wilkie Collins. [In preparation.]"
Another reference to the fact that she was
writing the biography is a note in Howard
Haycraft's Murder for Pleasure, which
indicates that Alexander Woolcott also knew
of the project. If Miss Sayers ever did complete
the work, it was never published.

III. Book Reviews

G42. "Charles Williams," Time and Tide, (December 2,
        1950), p.1220.
        Miss Sayers reviews two reprints of Williams'
books: He Came Down From Heaven and The Forgiveness
of Sins (1 volume), and The Region of the Summer
Stars.
G43. "The Technique of the Sermon," The Spectator,
        Vol.164 (February 2, 1940), p.150.
        This article is a review of the book: The
Art of Preaching by Charles Smyth, which was
published in London: S.P.C.K., 1940. Miss Sayers

discusses the message of the book and is
quite favorable in her opinion of its value.

IV. Children's Books

G44. The Days of Christ's Coming.

> London: H. Hamilton, 1953; 1960.
>   unpaged ₍4p.₎ (Illustrated)
> New York: Harper, 1960.   unpaged ₍28p.₎
>   (Illustrated)

A retelling of the story of the birth of
Christ and up to the flight into Egypt. The
exquisite medieval-style illustrations were
done by Fritz Wegner in multicolor combinations
and in brown and white. As a children's book,
it is suitable for ages five to ten. See also
(G64).

G45. Even the Parrot: Exemplary Conversations for
    Enlightened Children.

> London: Methuen, 1944.   55p. (Illustrated)

It is a little difficult to know where to
place this collection of children's stories.
The author's sub-title gives a hint of the
early nineteenth-century manner in which the
stories are written. Miss Sayers herself describes

them as a protest against, or a questioning
of, the creed of enlightened humanism, under
which heading she includes the topics of fresh
air during sleep, the underground building
of factories, the regulation of eating, and the
future place of the male in society! The parody
is invariably amusing. Miss Sayers must have
had good fun in writing it, and most of its
readers will have equally good fun in doing
their share. But it is to be hoped that if
there is any disposition to take it seriously,
somebody will comfort Nurse Nature not with too
well-mannered young charges, but with someone
more worthy of her steel. (Adapted from a
review in the Times Literary Supplement
(November 25, 1944), p.574.) The illustrations
are by Sillince.

V. Edited Series

G46. Bridgeheads. Edited by Dorothy L. Sayers and
      Muriel St. Clare Byrne, 1941-1946.   3v.
      According to the Manchester Guardian,
(August 1, 1941), p.3, this series was supposed

to "interpret a new and very radical
attitude to life which the editors discern
on the horizons of the near future." The
three volumes comprising this series are:

Sayers, Dorothy L. The Mind of the Maker.
London: Methuen, 1941.   186p. (C92).

Ellis-Fermor, Una Mary. Masters of Reality.
London: Methuen, 1942.   138p. (G46a).

Herbert, Alan Patrick. The Point of
Parliament. London: Methuen, 1946.
111p. (G46b).

VI. Letters

G47. "Charles Williams," Times [London] (May 14, 1955),
p.9e.

A letter written by C.S. Lewis and Dorothy
L. Sayers announcing the tenth anniversary of
the death of Charles Williams. They urge his
disciples and students to pay tribute at the
meetings to be held in London, Oxford, and
Cambridge.

G48. "Chekhov at the Westminster," New Statesman
and Nation, Vol.13 (February 27, 1937),
p.324.

A letter in which Miss Sayers disagrees
with a review given by Desmond McCarthy of
Uncle Vanya. Miss Sayers, in effect, gives
her own review of the play.

G49. "Dogma or Doctrine?" The Spectator, Vol.165
(July 19, 1940), p.62.

A letter commenting upon another letter
from Dr. W.B. Selbie, regarding the subject of
dogma and doctrine.

G50. A letter to Michael Gilbert. In: Brean, Herbert,
ed. The Mystery Writer's Handbook. New
York: Harper, 1956.

This letter is contained in a chapter
entitled "Technicalese" on pages 64 and 65.
It regards the author's work on The Nine Tailors
for the most part.

G51. A letter to the editor of the Evening Standard,
January 7, 1939.

This is another of the letters contributing
to the controversy which arose out of Howard
Spring's review of Agatha Christie's book

<u>Murder</u> <u>for</u> <u>Christmas</u>. He apparently removed every element of the mystery, revealing the identity of the murderer, the motive, how the murder was done, and how the detective knew it. Sayers explains by example how a reviewer should review detective stories without giving away the plot. An interesting article on the whole controversy is Clarence Boutell's "England's Other Crisis," <u>Publisher's</u> <u>Weekly</u>, Vol.135 (April 15, 1939), pp.1426-29. Sayers' letter was reprinted in Boutell's article (p.1427), and in <u>The</u> <u>Saturday</u> <u>Review</u> <u>of</u> <u>Literature</u>, Vol.25 (December 19, 1942), p.13.

G52. A letter to <u>The</u> <u>Listener</u>, in which Miss Sayers alludes to an earlier broadcast on the B.B.C. on the re-uniting of the body and the spirit.

See <u>The</u> <u>Listener</u>, Vol.44 (November 23, 1950), p.594. For responses to Sayers, see pages 547, 594-95 and 647. The original essay and broadcast was entitled: "The New Cosmology."

G53. Letters. <u>John</u> <u>O'</u> <u>London's</u> <u>Weekly</u>, Vol.51 (April 7, 1944), p.16; Vol.51 (May 19, 1944), pp.77-78.

These letters form part of a correspondence between Miss Sayers and Frederick Laws.

G54. "Mr. Winston Churchill," _Time_ _and_ _Tide_,

      Vol.21 (October 26, 1940), p.1044.

      Obviously, a letter expressing the

  author's thoughts about the Prime Minister.

G55. "Projects at School," _Times_ (November 26, 1952),

      p.9e.

      A letter apparently in response to an article

on school projects. Sayers wants to make note

of the fact that students who are unwilling

to do work for themselves are not peculiar to

England. She goes on to describe the requests

made to her by students in America supposedly

doing "research" on her works.

G56. "Religious Education," _Times_ (August 26, 1941),

      p.5e.

      A letter expressing her views on religious

education in wartime.

G57. "St. Anne's Church, Soho," _Times_ (August 8,

      1953), p.9a.

      A letter written by the Rev. P. McLaughlin,

Rector, and Miss Sayers, Church-warden, appealing

for the restoration of the former Church of

St. Thomas, now to be called the Parish Church

of St. Anne.

G58. "Spitfire Funds," _Times_ (August 24, 1940),
p.5e.

A letter expressing her views on Spitfire
and Red Cross funds during the war, in response
to an article on same.

G59. "The Theatre in Time of War," _Times_ (September
6, 1939), p.4f.

Miss Sayers disagrees in this letter with
Sir Oswald Stoll who suggested that closing
theatres and leaving churches open is "illogical."
She notes a distinction between entertainment
and worship, and adds that religious services
are held during the day-time, "when the task
of removing people to shelter... is easier
than during the hours of evening performance."
This letter was written by Miss Sayers and
Helen Simpson, dated September 4, 1939, from
24 Great James Street.

G60. "_Troilus and Cressida_ at the Westminster," _Times_
(September 24, 1938), p.11d.

A letter on the timeliness of Shakespeare's
savagely bitter, "war-debunking" play: "If ever
there was a play for the time it is this."

G61. "Whither Wimsey?" <u>Times</u> (November 24, 1938),

      p.15e.

      Sayers answers an editorial of November 21,
1938, p.13e, in mild disapproval of her
permission to allow Lord Peter to appear in
an advertisement endorsing a product "for that
tired feeling." In her letter she notes that
this is not the peer's first excursion into
advertising, nor hers, she having worked as
a copywriter for nine years, and Lord Peter
having worked for Pym's for a short time (c.f.,
<u>Murder</u> <u>Must</u> <u>Advertise</u>). She adds that her
copy was altered by the advertisers and, therefore, was "not up to Peter's standard" nor hers.
Sayers further explains that, having committed
as much as she could from her bank account to
further a provincial tour of <u>The</u> <u>Zeal</u> <u>of</u> <u>Thy</u>
<u>House</u>, she decided to enlist Mammon once more
in the service of the Church. The controversy
continues, in Latin for the most part, with a
letter from H.E. Calvan (November 26, 1938),
p.13e, and a reply from Sayers, "Et Laudavit
Dominus," (November 30, 1938), p.15e.

G62. "The Wimsey Chin," _Times_ (December 4, 1937),
p.15e.

A letter signed "Matthew Wimsey, i.e.,
Dorothy L. Sayers," commenting upon and
answering a reference (whose is not clear)
to the weakness of the Wimsey jaw. On the
contrary, Lord Peter has a "long, narrow
chin, and a long, receding forehead.... Labour
papers, softening down the chin, caracatured
him as a typical aristocrat" (c.f., _Whose Body?_)

VII. Pamphlets

G63. An Account of Lord Mortimer Wimsey, the Hermit
of the Wash, Related in a Letter to Sir
H--- G---bart, by a Clergyman of the Church
of England... Bristol; Printed by M. Bryan,
Corn-street, 1816. ₎i.e., London: Oxford
University Press, 1938.₎   13p.

A spoof booklet, printed in an edition of
250 copies for private distribution. The
clergyman relates soberly the sad consequences
of Enthusiasm upon the life of a brother of the
Duke of Denver. (See Sandoe). In a letter to

Miss Burger from Mr. Harry Carter of Oxford
University Press, 250 copies of this pamphlet
with the collation: 15 pages, Demy 8vo,
December 1937, were printed to the order of
Mr. Graham Pollard, owner of the firm of
Birrell & Garnett Ltd. until 1938. He was
apparently a dealer in rare and old books.
Delivery was made on December 21, 1937.
(Mr. Pollard was a close friend of the Printer
to the University.) The Bodleian Library has
a copy of the pamphlet, dated 1937 (shelfmark
25613 d.130). Since Mr. Sandoe lists this work
as being published in 1938, he possibly obtained
his information in a letter from Miss Sayers in
January of 1944.

G64. The Days of Christ's Coming. The Picture
Painted by Fritz Wegner. London: Hamish
Hamilton, 1953. [unpaged?]

This is one of three Christmas card texts
by Miss Sayers. They are actually called this
because they are literally in Christmas card
format, printed on 8½" x 11" card stock and
beautifully illustrated by Fritz Wegner. This
consists of three pages of text. Around 30,000
copies were printed for general distribution. See (G44).

G65. The Greatest Drama Ever Staged. London:
Hodder & Stoughton, 1939.   44p.;
London: Falcon Booklets, 1964.   16p.
Includes the essay: "The Triumph of
Easter." See (C83).

G66. The Image in the Mirror. London: Todd Publishing
Co., 1943.   16p. (Polybooks)
First published as a short story. See (B17).

G67. The Incredible Elopement of Lord Peter Wimsey.
London: Todd Publishing Co., 1943.   16p.
(Polybooks)
First published as a short story. See (B19).

G68. The Lost Tools of Learning. London: Methuen,
1948.   30p.
Published also as an essay; see (C49) and
(C145). Also given as a speech; see (G24).

G69. The Mysterious English. London: Macmillan,
1941.   31p.; New York: Macmillan, 1941.
31p. (On cover: Macmillan war pamphlets,
no.10)
First given as a speech; see (G27). Also
published in essay form; see (C53).

G70. The Other Six Deadly Sins. London: Methuen,
1943.   31p.
First delivered as a speech; see (G30). Also

published as an essay; see (C59).

G71. The Story of Adam and Christ. The Verses
Written by D.L. Sayers, the Window
Painted by Fritz Wegner. London: Hamish
Hamilton, 1953.   (folio) [unpaged?]

This is one of three Christmas card texts
by Miss Sayers. They are printed, in Christmas
card format, on 8½" x 11" card stock and
beautifully illustrated by Fritz Wegner. This
consists of two pages of text. Approximately
30,000 were printed for general distribution.

G72. The Story of Noah's Ark. Retold by D.L. Sayers.
The Picture Painted by Fritz Wegner. London:
Hamish Hamilton, 1956.   [unpaged?]

This is one of three Christmas card texts
by Miss Sayers printed in Christmas card format
on 8½" x 11" card stock and beautifully
illustrated by Fritz Wegner. It consists of
three pages of text. Approximately 30,000 copies
were printed for general distribution.

G73. Strong Meat. London: Hodder & Stoughton, 1939.
44p.

Includes the essay: "The Dogma is the Drama."
See (C28) and (C105).

G74. The Unsolved Puzzle of the Man with No Face.

    London: Todd Publishing Co., 1943.

    16p. (Polybooks)

    First published as a short story. See (B43).

G75. Why Work? An Address Delivered at Eastbourne,

    April 23rd, 1942. London: Methuen, 1942.

    24p.

    As an address, see (G39); as an essay,

see (C88).

G76. Wimsey, Matthew [pseud.] i.e., Dorothy L.

    Sayers. Papers Relating to the Family of

    Wimsey. Edited by Matthew Wimsey. [On

    the fictional family in Dorothy L. Sayers'

    detective novels. With plates.] London:

    Privately Printed for the Family by

    Humphrey Milford, 1935.   55p.

    Sayers, in a letter to P.M. Stone, December

12, 1943, identifies the editor as "Miss Helen

Simpson and myself." Contributors to this

"spoof booklet" (the words are Sayers') include

the late Miss Simpson, Muriel St. Clare Byrne,

Mr. N.M. Smither, and Mr. and Mrs. Scott-Giles.

    The pamphlet traces the tempestuous romance

of Lord St. George, eldest son of the 10th Duke

of Denver, who married the widow of a
hosier and involved himself in his father's
considerable wrath. (See Sandoe).

In a letter to Miss Burger dated June 5,
1976, Muriel St. Clare Byrne states that this
work was actually published in December 1936,
and that her own copy is dated by Miss Sayers,
December 16, 1936. The publication date given
above is that listed in the British Museum's
General Catalogue of Printed Books, 1966-70
Supplement.

Section H

CRITICISM

For the purpose of organization those items
of a critical or discoursive nature about Dorothy
L. Sayers and her writings are arranged into four
areas. The first of these are articles that concern
her entirely. A second area concerns three
dissertations written about her works. The third
area consists of materials which in part cover
Miss Sayers along with other writers. The fourth
and last area is a listing of reviews, many of
which express critical comment.

I. <u>Articles</u>

  H1. Basney, Lionel. "God and Peter Wimsey,"
       <u>Christianity</u> <u>Today</u>, Vol.17 (September
       14, 1973), pp. 27-28.
       An interesting discussion of Sayers'
     religious tendencies and her detective fiction.

H2. Green, Martin. "The Detection of a Snob,"
   The Listener, Vol.49 (March 14, 1963),
   pp.461, 464.

   A general discussion of Miss Sayers and her
detective novels.

H3. Grella, George. "Dorothy Sayers and Peter
   Wimsey," The University of Rochester
   Library Bulletin, Vol.28 (Summer, 1974),
   pp.33-42.

   A rather critical survey of Sayers as a
detective fiction writer and the worth of
Lord Peter as a detective.

H4. Harrison, Barbara Grizutti. "Dorothy L. Sayers
   and the Tidy Art of Detective Fiction,"
   Ms., Vol.3 (November, 1974), pp.66-69,
   85-89.

   A discussion of Sayers as feminist in
relation to the Wimsey-Vane trilogy: Strong
Poison, Gaudy Night, and Busman's Honeymoon.

H5. Heilbrun, Carolyn. "Sayers, Lord Peter and God,"
   The American Scholar, Vol.37 (Spring, 1968),
   pp.324-330+

   An excellent treatment of the career of
Dorothy L. Sayers, both biographical and critical.

H6. Leavis, Q.D. "The Case of Miss Dorothy Sayers,"
     Scrutiny, Vol.6 (December, 1937), pp.334-340.

     A general discussion of Miss Sayers as a
detective fiction writer, along with reviews
of the novels: _Gaudy Night_ and _Busman's Honeymoon_.

H7. Rickman, H.P. "From Detection to Theology: The
     Work of Dorothy Sayers," _Hibbert Journal_,
     Vol.60 (July, 1962), pp.290-296.

     A good discussion of the transition of Miss
Sayers as a writer of detective fiction to that
of theology.

H8. Soper, David Wesley. "Dorothy Sayers and the
     Christian Synthesis," _Religion in Life_,
     Vol.21 (1951), pp.117-128.

     Discusses the role of Miss Sayers as a
Christian writer.

H9. Thurmer, John. "The Theology of Dorothy L.
     Sayers," _Church Quarterly Review_, Vol.168
     (October-December, 1967), pp.452-462.

     Discusses Miss Sayers' theological concepts
as expressed in her writings in this topic.

H10. Webster, Deborah. "Reinterpreter: Dorothy L.
     Sayers," _Catholic World_, Vol.169 (August,
     1949), pp.330-335.

A discussion of Miss Sayers' Anglo-
Catholic thought including some background
material on her life as a detective fiction
writer.

II. <u>Dissertations</u>

H11. Burleson, James Bernard, Jr. "A Study of the
Novels of Dorothy L. Sayers," (unpublished
dissertation) The University of Texas,
1965.   232ℓ.
For a copy of the Abstract see <u>Dissertation</u>
<u>Abstracts</u>, Vol.26, p.2204. "The object of
this dissertation is to analyze and evaluate
the achievement of Dorothy Sayers as a detective
novelist." (From the Abstract)

H12. Fairman, Marion Baker. "The Neo-Medieval Plays
of Dorothy L. Sayers," (unpublished
dissertation) University of Pittsburgh,
1961.   200ℓ.
For a copy of the Abstract see <u>Dissertation</u>
<u>Abstracts</u>, Vol.23, p.1016. "Dorothy L. Sayers'
plays are analyzed to determine if her renewed
artistic enthusiasm for the medieval dramatic

forms indicates a redirected interest in
matters of faith and theology as a means
of examining and expanding the man of the
modern world." (From the Abstract)

H13. Soloway, Sara Lee. "Dorothy Sayers: Novelist,"
(unpublished dissertation) University
of Kentucky, 1971.   363ℓ.

For a copy of the Abstract see <u>Dissertation</u>
<u>Abstracts</u>, Vol.32, p.2105-A. "This study
approaches Miss Sayers' Wimsey series in
terms of the idea that the author is a
sophisticated theorist who, conscious of the
major problems involved in writing in the
detective <u>genre</u>, nevertheless insists that
detective fiction can indeed be considered
as part of the mainstream of literature." (From
the Abstract)

III. <u>Interpretations</u>

H14. Acocella, Joan R. "The Cult of Language: A
Study of Two Modern Translations of Dante,"
<u>Modern Language Quarterly</u>, Vol.35 (June,
1974), pp.140-156.

The author compares Miss Sayers'
translation of Dante to that of John Ciardi.

H15. Brazun, Jacques. _A Catalogue of Crime_. With
Wendell H. Taylor. New York: Harper &
Row, 1971.   831p.

A considerable number of references are
made to Sayers. Her novels are critically
discussed on pages 374-376+.

H16. Bentley, E.C. "Greedy Night," reprinted in
Dorothy L. Sayers' _Lord Peter; A Collection
of All the Lord Peter Wimsey Stories_, edited
by James Sandoe. New York: Harper & Row,
1972.

This article appears on pages 447-464. It
is an hilarious parody of _Gaudy Night_, Sayers,
Lord Peter, and Bunter, in general.

H17. Bergin, Thomas G. _Dante_. New York: The Orion
Press, 1965.

At various places Bergin discusses Miss
Sayers in relation to her work on Dante.

H18. Cawelti, John G. _Adventure, Mystery, and Romance;
Formula Stories as Art and Popular Culture_.
Chicago: University of Chicago Press, 1976.
344p.

Includes a discussion of Sayers' novel
<u>The</u> <u>Nine</u> <u>Tailors</u>.

H19. Clark, Barrett, H., ed. <u>A</u> <u>History</u> <u>of</u> <u>Modern</u>
<u>Drama</u>. With George Freedley. New York:
D. Appleton-Century Co., 1947.   832p.
Discusses Miss Sayers' dramatic works.
See page 216.

H20. Cunningham, Gilbert F. <u>The</u> <u>Divine</u> <u>Comedy</u> <u>in</u>
<u>English</u>; <u>A</u> <u>Critical</u> <u>Bibliography</u>, <u>1901-1966</u>.
New York: Barnes & Noble, 1965-66; c1966.
2v.
Sayers is covered on pages 211-220 in
volume two.

H21. Curtayne, A. "Dante," <u>Studies</u>, Vol.54 (Summer-
Fall, 1965), pp.217-226.
Includes a discussion of Miss Sayers'
translations of <u>The</u> <u>Divine</u> <u>Comedy</u>.

H22. "Departure from Crime," <u>Newsweek</u>, Vol.46
(August 22, 1955), pp.82-83.
Discusses Sayers as a scholar and theologian.

H23. "Everyday Dogma," <u>Time</u>, Vol.53 (May 30, 1949),
p.56+
Discusses some of Sayers' religious views.

H24. "For an Evening Service," <u>Christian</u> <u>Century</u>,
        Vol.71 (November 3, 1954), p.1329.

    Includes a discussion of Miss Sayers'
theological views.

H25. Gilbert, Michael. "Technicalese," <u>The</u> <u>Mystery</u>
        <u>Writer's</u> <u>Handbook</u>, edited by Herbert Brean.
        New York: Harper, 1956, pp.57-65.

    Gilbert discusses Sayers' use of "technicalese"
in <u>The</u> <u>Nine</u> <u>Tailors</u> and <u>Unnatural</u> <u>Death</u>, but
most noteworthy is a lengthy excerpt from a
letter written by Miss Sayers to Gilbert
regarding her work on <u>The</u> <u>Nine</u> <u>Tailors</u>.

H26. Haycraft, Howard, ed. <u>The</u> <u>Art</u> <u>of</u> <u>the</u> <u>Mystery</u>
        <u>Story</u>; <u>A</u> <u>Collection</u> <u>of</u> <u>Critical</u> <u>Essays</u>.
        New York: Simon & Schuster, 1946.

    Includes two essays by Sayers, "The Omnibus
of Crime," (C94) and "Gaudy Night," (C38), as
well as numerous references made to her by the
other contributors.

H27. Haycraft, Howard. <u>Murder</u> <u>for</u> <u>Pleasure</u>; <u>The</u> <u>Life</u>
        <u>and</u> <u>Times</u> <u>of</u> <u>the</u> <u>Detective</u> <u>Story</u>. New
        York: D. Appleton-Century, 1941.

    On pages 135-142, Haycraft discusses Miss
Sayers' contribution to detective fiction

writing. A check of the index reveals some
twenty-one other references to Sayers.

H28. "Is the Detective Story Dead? A Recorded
Dialogue Between Julian Symons and
Edmund Crispin," _Times Literary Supplement_,
(June 23, 1961), p.iv.

In this discussion or dialogue Miss Sayers
and some of her works are mentioned.

H29. Johnston, R.C. "Hoese Boot in the Chanson de
Roland, Line 641," _Modern Language Review_,
Vol.58 (July, 1963), pp.391-2.

Includes a discussion of Sayers' translation
of _The Song of Roland_.

H30. Larmoth, Jeanine. _Murder on the Menu; Recipes
by Charlotte Turgeon._ New York: Scribner's,
1972.

Larmoth mentions Lord Peter Wimsey, Bunter,
and Miss Sayers many times throughout this work.

H31. Mascall, E.L. _The Secularization of Christianity;
An Analysis and Critique_. New York: Holt,
Rinehart, & Winston, 1966, c1965.

At various points in this book, Mascall
mentions Miss Sayers' theological writings.

H32. Mochrie, M. "They Make Crime Pay," _Delineator_,
Vol.130 (February, 1937), p.28.

Includes some information on Miss Sayers,
and also has a portrait and illustration.

H33. Murch, A.E. _The Development of the Detective_
Novel. New York: Philosophical Library,
1958.

In the chapter "The Golden Age," on pages
221-223+, Miss Sayers and her novels are
discussed.

H34. "Mystery Story," _Time_, Vol.69 (January 21, 1957),
p.36+

A reaction to her theological writings,
especially _The Great Mystery_. See (C121).

H35. Nott, Kathleen. "Lord Peter Views the Soul," in
her _Emperor's Clothes_. London: Heinemann,
1954, pp.253-298.

A rather lengthy dissertation on the
differences between Miss Sayers' theological
and fictional writings.

H36. Portugal, Eustace. "Death to Detectives,"
Bookman (London), Vol.84 (April, 1933),
p.28.

Includes a discussion of Lord Peter Wimsey
as a Sayers characterization.

H37. Raymond, J. "White Tile or Red Plush?" New
Statesman and Nation, Vol.51 (June 30,
1956), p.756+

Discusses Sayers. Reply: S.M. Hall &
A.S. Hall in Vol.52 (July 14, 1956), p.43.

H38. Simonds, K. "Bloodhound into Bridegroom,"
Saturday Review of Literature, Vol.18
(Septemebr 3, 1938), p.14.

Actually a review of the combined editions
of The Documents in the Case and Clouds of
Witness; Murder Must Advertise and Hangman's
Holiday; The Dawson Pedigree and Lord Peter
Views the Body. The discussion is a general
one about Miss Sayers as a writer of detective
fiction.

H39. Spanos, William V. "The Canterbury History:
Figural Imitation," in his Christian
Tradition in Modern British Verse Drama:
The Poetics of Sacramental Time. New
Brunswick, N.J.: Rutgers University Press,
1967.

On pages 81-134+ there is a discussion of
all of Sayers' religious plays, especially
The Zeal of Thy House.

H40. Sprague, Rosamond Kent. "Introduction," in
Sayers, Dorothy L. _A Matter of Eternity;_
Selections from the Writings of Dorothy L.
Sayers. Oxford: A.R. Mowbray, 1973.   139p.

An interesting discussion of Miss Sayers'
religious thought.

H41. Strachey, John. "The Golden Age of English
Detection," _Saturday Review of Literature_,
Vol.19 (January 7, 1939), pp.12-14.

A brief comparison of the major detective
fiction writers of the period, including Miss
Sayers.

H42. Swinnerton, Frank. _The Georgian Literary Scene_,
1910-1935; A Panorama. London: Hutchinson,
1950.   415p.

Miss Sayers is discussed in various places
in this book, particularly on pages 341-343.

H43. Symons, Julian. _The Detective Story in Britain_.
London: Longmans, 1962.

On pages 26-28 there is a select bibliography
of works, along with critical and bibliographical
studies. Also includes a portrait.

H44. Symons, Julian. _Mortal Consequences; A History_
from the Detective Story to the Crime Novel.

New York: Harper & Row, 1972.

Miss Sayers and her works are refered
to many times in this work.

H45. "Translation," _Times Literary Supplement_,
(December 5, 1958), p.705.

Includes a discussion of Miss Sayers'
translation of _The Divine Comedy_.

H46. "Wanted: More and Better Theology," _Sower_,
Vol.141 (October, 1941), p.15.

Includes some mention of Miss Sayers'
theological views.

H47. Watson, Colin. _Snobbery with Violence; Crime
Stories and Their Audience_. London: Eyre
& Spottisoode, 1971.

A check of the index will reveal a number
of references to Miss Sayers, as well as the
chapter, "Girls Who Kept Cool."

H48. Weales, Gerald C. "Charles Williams and Dorothy
Sayers," in his _Religion in Modern English
Drama_. Philadelphia: University of Pennsylvania
Press, 1961.

On pages 142 to 179 is a discussion of
Sayers' religous plays.

H49. Wilson, Edmund. <u>A</u> <u>Literary</u> <u>Chronicle</u>: <u>1920-</u>
<u>1950</u>. Garden City, N.Y.: Doubleday Anchor
Books, 1956.   442p.

On pages 339 to 341, Mr. Wilson criticises
Miss Sayers' ability as a detective fiction
writer as exemplified in her novel <u>The</u> <u>Nine</u>
<u>Tailors</u>.

IV. Reviews

H50. <u>Are</u> <u>Women</u> <u>Human?</u>
<u>National</u> <u>Review</u>. Vol.24 (July 7, 1972),
p.751.

H51. <u>Begin</u> <u>Here</u>; <u>A</u> <u>Statement</u> <u>of</u> <u>Faith</u>
<u>Booklist</u>. Vol.37 (June 1, 1941), p.458.
<u>Bookmark</u>. Vol.2 (November, 1941), p.7.
<u>Books</u>. (May 4, 1941), p.11.
<u>Christian</u> <u>Century</u>. Vol.58 (May 14, 1941),
p.659.
<u>Christian</u> <u>Science</u> <u>Monitor</u>. (Septemebr 18,
1941), p.20.
<u>Churchman</u>. Vol.155 (June 1, 1941), p.35.
<u>Cleveland</u> <u>Open</u> <u>Shelf</u>. (May 1941), p.9.
<u>Foreign</u> <u>Affairs</u>. Vol.20 (January, 1942), p.378.

Hibbert Journal. Vol.66 (January, 1941), p.213.

Library Journal. Vol.66 (April 1, 1941), p.304.

Manchester Guardian. (February 2, 1940), p.3.

Nation. Vol.152 (May 10, 1941), p.561.

Nature. Vol.145 (May 25, 1940), p.815.

New Republic. Vol.105 (August 4, 1941), p.166.

New York Times Book Review. (May 18, 1941), p.8.

New Yorker. Vol.17 (May 3, 1941), p.85.

The Spectator. Vol.164 (February 9, 1940), p.187.

Springfield Republican. (May 15, 1941), p.12.

Survey. Vol.77 (December, 1941), p.371.

Times Literary Supplement. (January 27, 1940), p.48.

Wisconsin Library Bulletin. Vol.37 (June, 1941), p.114.

H52. Busman's Honeymoon

Booklist. Vol.33 (March, 1937), p.214.

Books. (February 28, 1937), p.19.

Boston Transcript. (February 20, 1937), p.4.

Canadian Forum. Vol.17 (April, 1937), p.30.

Christian Century. Vol.54 (March 3, 1937), p.291.

Manchester Guardian. (June 25, 1937), p.6.

New Republic. Vol.90 (March 24, 1937), p.219.

New Statesman and Nation. Vol.13 (June 26, 1937), p.1050.

New York Times Book Review. (February 21, 1937), p.22.

Pratt. (Summer, 1937), p.40.

Saturday Review of Literature. Vol.15 (February 20, 1937), p.18.

The Spectator. Vol.158 (June 18, 1937), p.1156.

Springfield Republican. (February 21, 1937), p.7e.

Times Literary Supplement. (June 12, 1937), p.445.

Wisconsin Library Bulletin. Vol.33 (April, 1937), p.87.

H53. Catholic Tales and Christian Songs (1918)

Catholic World. Vol.110 (October, 1919), p.108.

Nation. Vol.109 (September 27, 1919), p.441.

New York Evening Post, (November 1, 1919), p.2.

H54. Christian Letters to a Post-Christian World

Choice. Vol.6 (October, 1969), p.1030;

Vol.7 (November, 1970), p.1245.

Christian Century. Vol.86 (June 25, 1969),
p.877.

Library Journal. Vol.94 (August, 1969),
p.2795.

New York Times Book Review. (March 15,
1970), p.40.

H55. Clouds of Witness

Best Sellers. Vol.31 (September 1, 1971),
p.256.

Books (New York Herald Tribune). (May 1,
1927), p.11.

Boston Transcript. (June 11, 1927), p.4.

H56. Clouds ofWitness; and The Documents in the Case

Booklist. Vol.34 (July 15, 1938), p.401.

Boston Transcript. (July 30, 1938), p.1.

New York Times Book Review. (July 24, 1938),
p.12.

Saturday Review of Literature. Vol.18
(July 30, 1938), p.20; (September 3, 1938), p.14.

H57. Creed or Chaos?

Booklist. Vol.45 (March 15, 1949), p.233.

Catholic World. Vol.169 (August, 1949), p.330.

Chicago Sun. (March 2, 1949), [n.p.]

Christian Century. Vol.66 (April 13, 1949),
p.466.

Crozer Quarterly. Vol.26 (October, 1949),
p.374.

Kirkus Reviews. Vol.17 (February 1, 1949),
p.74.

New York Times Book Review. (May 29, 1949),
p.13.

New Yorker. Vol.25 (June 4, 1949), p.95.

Saturday Review of Literature. Vol32 (July 16,
1949), p.15.

The Spectator. Vol.178 (April 11, 1947),
p.410.

Times Literary Supplement. (May 31, 1947),
p.270.

H58. The Dawson Pedigree, i.e., Unnatural Death; and
Lord Peter Views the Body

Booklist. Vol.35 (September 15, 1938), p.29.

Saturday Review of Literature. Vol.18
(August 27, 1938), p.18; (September 3, 1938), p.14.

Wisconsin Library Bulletin. Vol.34 (December,
1938), p.201.

H59. The Days of Christ's Coming

Atlantic. Vol.206 (December, 1960), p.130.

Chicago Sunday Tribune. (December 4, 1960),
p.33.

Library Journal. Vol.85 (November 15, 1960), p.4218. (Two reviews)

New York Herald Tribune Lively Arts. (December 11, 1960), p.39.

New York Times Book Review. (December 4, 1960), p.66.

San Francisco Chronicle. (November 13, 1960), p.17.

Times Literary Supplement. (November 25, 1960), p.xvii.

H60. The Devil to Pay

Booklist. Vol.36 (December 1, 1939), p.130.

Books. (November 12, 1939), p.38.

Christian Century. Vol.56 (October 4, 1939), p.1211.

Churchman. Vol.153 (November 15, 1939), p.18.

Commonweal. Vol.31 (January 19, 1940), p.290.

Manchester Guardian. (July 14, 1939), p.9.

New Statesman and Nation. Vol.18 (July 29, 1938), p.177.

Springfield Republican. (October 8, 1939), p.7e.

Theatre Arts Monthly. Vol.23 (October, 1939), pp.706-7.

Times <u>Literary</u> <u>Supplement</u>. (June 17,
1939), p.353.

H61. <u>The</u> <u>Documents</u> <u>in</u> <u>the</u> <u>Case</u>

<u>Booklist</u>. Vol.27 (June, 1931), p.456.

<u>Bookman</u>. Vol.73 (June, 1931), p.xv.

<u>Books</u>. (April 19, 1931), p.14.

<u>Boston</u> <u>Transcript</u>. (June 10, 1931), p.2.

<u>Nation</u> <u>and</u> <u>Athaneum</u>. Vol.47 (August 9, 1930),
p.597.

<u>New</u> <u>York</u> <u>Times</u> <u>Book</u> <u>Review</u>. (April 19, 1931),
p.13.

<u>Outlook</u>. Vol.158 (May 27, 1931), p.121.

<u>Saturday</u> <u>Review</u> <u>of</u> <u>Literature</u>. Vol.7 (July
18, 1931), p.981.

<u>The</u> <u>Spectator</u>. Vol.145 (October 11, 1930),
p.504.

<u>Springfield</u> <u>Republican</u>. (June 21, 1931),
p.7e.

Times <u>Literary</u> <u>Supplement</u>. (July 17, 1930),
p.594.

H62. <u>Emperor</u> <u>Constantine</u>; <u>A</u> <u>Chronicle</u>

<u>American</u> <u>Ecclesiastical</u> <u>Review</u>. Vol.127
(December, 1952), pp.479-480.

<u>Booklist</u>. Vol.48 (June 15, 1952), p.335.

Christian Century. Vol.69 (June 18, 1952), p.724.

Churchman. Vol.166 (November 1, 1952), p.17.

Commonweal. Vol.56 (July 4, 1952), p.326.

Interpretation. Vol.7 (January, 1953), pp.120-121.

Kirkus Reviews. Vol.20 (June 15, 1952), p.345.

Wisconsin Library Bulletin. Vol.48 (July, 1952), p.170.

H63. Even the Parrot

Times Literary Supplement. (November 25, 1944), p.574.

H64. Five Red Herrings (U.S.: Suspicious Characters)

Booklist. Vol.28 (November, 1931), p.106.

Bookman. Vol.74 (November, 1931), p.xv.

Books. (September 20, 1931), p.14.

Boston Transcript. (September 20, 1931), p.14.

Chicago Daily Tribune. (September 19, 1931), p.13.

New York Times Book Review. (September 13, 1931), p.21.

Outlook. Vol.159 (September 23, 1931), p.123.

Saturday Review. Vol.151 (March 7, 1931),
p.347.

The Spectator. Vol.146 (May 9, 1931),
p.746.

Times Literary Supplement. (April 9, 1931),
p.290.

H65. Further Papers on Dante

Blackfriars. Vol.38 (October, 1937),
pp.426-230.

Catholic World. Vol.186 (February, 1958),
p.398.

Commonweal. Vol.66 (August 23, 1957), p.524.

Library Journal. Vol.82 (September 1, 1957),
p.2030.

New York Times Book Review. (September 22,
1957), p.29.

Saturday Review of Literature. Vol.40
(November 9, 1957), p.44.

Studies. Vol.46 (Winter, 1957), p.493.

Tablet. Vol.210 (July 13, 1957), p.38.

H66. Gaudy Night

Booklist. Vol.32 (March, 1936), p.202.

Books. (February 23, 1936), p.10.

Canadian Forum. Vol.15 (March, 1936), p.30.

Chicago Daily Tribune. (February 29, 1936), p.8.

Nation. Vol.142 (April 8, 1936), p.458.

New Republic. Vol.86 (March 11, 1936), p.147.

New Statesman and Nation. Vol.10 (November 16, 1935), p.740.

New York Times Book Review. (February 23, 1936), p.20.

Pratt. (Summer, 1936), p.38.

Publishers Weekly. Vol.193 (June 10, 1968), p.63.

Review of Research. Vol.93 (April, 1936), p.21.

Saturday Review of Literature. Vol.13 (February 22, 1936), p.6.

The Spectator. Vol.155 (November 15, 1935), p.828.

Springfield Republican. (March 8, 1936), p.7e.

Time. Vol.27 (February 24, 1936), p.75.

Times Literary Supplement. (November 9, 1935), p.719.

Wisconsin Library Bulletin. Vol.32 (April, 1936), p.50.

H67. The Greatest Drama Ever Staged

      Blackfriars. Vol.19 (August, 1938),
p.627.

H68. Hangman's Holiday

      Books. (September 24, 1933), p.22.

      New Statesman & Nation. Vol.5 (May 20,
1933), p.654.

      New York Evening Post. (September 30, 1933),
p.16.

      New York Times Book Review. (September 24,
1933), p.25.

      Saturday Review. Vol.155 (May 13, 1933),
p.461.

      Saturday Review of Literature. Vol.10
(September 23, 1933), p.136.

      Times Literary Supplement. (May 11, 1933),
p.328.

H69. Have His Carcase

      Booklist. Vol.28 (July, 1932), p.476.

      Books. (May 29, 1932), p.10.

      New Statesman and Nation. Vol.3 (May 7, 1932),
p.594.

      New York Evening Post. (May 21, 1932), p.7.

      New York Times Book Review. (May 29, 1932), p.10.

Saturday Review. Vol.153 (April 16, 1932),
p.396.

Saturday Review of Literature. Vol.8
(June 18, 1932), p.796.

The Spectator. Vol.148 (June 18, 1932),
p.874.

Springfield Republican. (May 29, 1932), p.7e.

Times Literary Supplement. (May 5, 1932),
p.333.

H70. In the Teeth of the Evidence, and Other Stories

Atlantic. (April, 1940), [n.p.]

Booklist. Vol.36 (March 15, 1940), p.284.

Books. (February 18, 1940), p.12.

Boston Transcript. (February 17, 1940), p.2.

Christian Century. Vol.57 (May 29, 1940),
p.706.

Manchester Guardian. (December 1, 1939),
p. supp. xiv.

New Republic. Vol.102 (February 19, 1940),
p.253.

New Statesman and Nation. Vol.18 (December 23,
1939), p.936.

New York Times Book Review. (February 18,
1940), p.23.

New Yorker. Vol.16 (February 17, 1940),
p.84.

Saturday Review of Literature. Vol.21
(February 17, 1940), p.18.

The Spectator. Vol.163 (December 15, 1939),
p.880.

Springfield Republican. (March 31, 1940),
p.7e.

Times Literary Supplement. (November 18,
1939), p.675.

H71. Introductory Papers on Dante

America. Vol.93 (September 3, 1955), p.539.

Blackfriars. Vol.36 (March, 1955), p.87.

Booklist. Vol.51 (July 15, 1955), p.464.

Catholic World. Vol.181 (September, 1955),
p.477.

Commonweal. Vol.62 (August 5, 1955), p.452.

Expository Times. Vol.67 (January, 1956),
pp.109-110.

Dublin Review. Vol.229 (Winter, 1955), p.482.

Jubilee. Vol.3 (June, 1955), p.58.

Kirkus Reviews. Vol.23 (June 1, 1955), p.382.

Library Journal. Vol.80 (June 15, 1955), p.1499.

Month. Vol.13 (March, 1955), p.185.

Nation. Vol.181 (December 17, 1955), p.540.

New Republic. Vol.133 (August 22, 1955), p.18.

New York Herald Tribune Book Review. (June 12, 1955), p.9.

New York Times Book Review. (May 29, 1955), p.7.

Tablet. Vol.205 (February 19, 1955), p.182.

Thought. Vol.31 (Autumn, 1956), p.462.

Times Literary Supplement. (December 17, 1954), p.823.

H72. The Just Vengeance

Blackfriars. Vol.28 (February, 1947), p.88.

Month. Vol.182 (September, 1946), p.387-388.

H73. Lord Peter; A Collection of All the Lord Peter Wimsey Stories

Book World. Vol.6 (July 16, 1972), p.14.

Booklist. Vol.68 (February 15, 1972), p.489; Vol.70 (February 1, 1974), p.573.

Kirkus Reviews. Vol.39 (December 1, 1971), p.1282.

Library Journal. Vol.97 (March 1, 1972), p.904.

New York Times Book Review. (January 16, 1972), p.42.

H74. <u>Lord</u> <u>Peter</u> <u>Views</u> <u>the</u> <u>Body</u>

<u>Bookman</u>. Vol.69 (May, 1929), p.xxvi.

<u>Books</u>. ⌈New York Herald Tribune⌉ (March 31, 1929), p.11.

<u>The</u> <u>Spectator</u>. Vol.141 (December 8, 1928), p.896.

<u>Times</u> <u>Literary</u> <u>Supplement</u>. (December 6, 1928), p.968.

H75. <u>Love</u> <u>All</u>

<u>New</u> <u>Statesman</u> <u>and</u> <u>Nation</u>. Vol.19 (April 13, 1940), p.493.

H76. <u>The</u> <u>Man</u> <u>Born</u> <u>to</u> <u>Be</u> <u>King</u>

<u>Blackfriars</u>. Vol.24 (November, 1943), pp.425-428.

<u>Booklist</u>. Vol.46 (December 15, 1949), p.139.

<u>Christian</u> <u>Century</u>. Vol.66 (November 30, 1949), p.1424.

<u>Churchman</u>. Vol.163 (December 15, 1949), p.16.

<u>Clergy</u> <u>Review</u>. ⌈n.s.⌉ Vol.23 (September, 1943), pp.417-419.

<u>Kirkus</u> <u>Reviews</u>. Vol.17 (October 1, 1949), p.543.

<u>Library</u> <u>Journal</u>. Vol.74 (October 15, 1949), p.1605.

Month. Vol.179 (May-June, 1943), pp.233-234.

New Statesman and Nation. Vol.26 (July 10, 1943), p.28.

New York Herald Tribune Book Review (November 13, 1949), p.38.

New York Times Book Review. (October 23, 1949), p.49.

Wisconsin Library Bulletin. (November, 1949), p.5.

H77. A Matter of Eternity

America. Vol.128 (May 12, 1973), p.447.

Choice. Vol.10 (November, 1973), p.1406.

H78. The Mind of the Maker

America. Vol.67 (May 9, 1942), p.133.

Blackfriars. Vol.22 (October, 1941), pp.562-563.

Booklist. Vol.38 (March 1, 1942), p.225.

Books. (March 1, 1942), p.23.

Catholic Arts Quarterly. Vol.21 (Christmas, 1957), pp.28-31.

Catholic World. Vol.165 (May, 1947), pp.159-162.

Churchman. Vol.156 (March 1, 1942), p.17.

Commonweal. Vol.35 (March 27, 1942), p.572.

Hibbert Journal. Vol.40 (January, 1942), p.202.

Journal of Bible and Religion. Vol.25 (October, 1957), pp.378-379.

Journal of Philosophy. Vol.39 (May 21, 1942), p.307.

Manchester Guardian. (August 1, 1941), p.3.

Moslem World. Vol.35 (January, 1945), pp.1-5.

Nation. Vol.154 (February 21, 1942), p.238.

New York Times Book Review. (September 27, 1942), p.29.

The Spectator. Vol.167 (August 22, 1941), p.190.

Springfield Republican. (February 15, 1942), p.7e.

Tablet. Vol.179 (January 10, 1942), p.20.

Times Literary Supplement. (August 9, 1941), p.382.

H79. Murder Must Advertise

Best Sellers. Vol.31 (February 1, 1972), p.496.

Booklist. Vol.29 (July, 1933), p.343.

Books. (April 9, 1933), p.17.

New Statesman and Nation. Vol.5 (March 18, 1933), p. supp. 342.

New York Evening Post. (April 8, 1933), p.7.

New York Times Book Review. (April 9, 1933), p.12.

Publishers Weekly. Vol.192 (August 7, 1967), p.57.

Saturday Review of Literature. Vol.9 (April 22, 1933), p.553; (May 6, 1933), p.581.

The Spectator. Vol.150 (February 17, 1933), p.224.

Springfield Republican. (April 9, 1933), p.7e.

Times Literary Supplement. (March 2, 1933), p.149.

Wisconsin Library Bulletin. Vol.29 (May, 1933), p.139.

H80. The Nine Tailors

Best Sellers. Vol.26 (December 15, 1966), p.354.

Booklist. Vol.30 (May, 1934), p.280.

Books. (March 25, 1934), p.18.

Boston Transcript. (April 21, 1934), p.2.

Forum. Vol.91 (May, 1934), p.vii.

New Statesman and Nation. Vol.7 (January 20, 1934), p.94.

New York Times Book Review. (March 25, 1934), p.11.

Pratt. (Summer, 1934), p.42.

Publishers Weekly. Vol.190 (August 1, 1966), p.62.

Saturday Review of Literature. Vol.10 (March 24, 1934), p.573, 581.

Springfield Republican. (March 25, 1934), p.7e; (April 1, 1934), p.7e.

Times Literary Supplement. (January 11,
1934), p.26.

Wisconsin Library Bulletin. Vol.30
(May, 1934), p.115.

H81. Omnibus

Books. (September 30, 1934), p.16.

Chicago Daily Tribune. (October 6, 1934), p.20.

New York Times Book Review. (September 30,
1934), p.20.

Saturday Review. Vol.155 (March 25, 1933),
p.290.

Saturday Review of Literature. Vol.11
(September 29, 1934), p.144.

Springfield Republican. (October 7, 1934),
p.7e.

Wisconsin Library Bulletin. Vol.30 (December,
1934), p.242.

H82. Omnibus of Crime

Books. ₍New York Herald Tribune₎ (August 11,
1929), p.5.

Boston Transcript. (September 4, 1929), p.3.

New York Evening Post. (August 10, 1929), p.6m.

New York Times Book Review. (August 11, 1929),
p.2.

Outlook. Vol.153 (September 11, 1929), p.70.

Springfield Republican. (September 1, 1929), p.7e.

H83. The Poetry of Search and the Poetry of Statement
Choice. Vol.3 (May, 1966), p.204.

New Statesman and Nation. Vol.66 (November 1, 1963), p.621.

Times Literary Supplement. (September 13, 1963), p.690.

H84. Second Omnibus of Crime
Booklist. Vol.28 (March, 1932), p.310.

Bookman. Vol.75 (June, 1932), p.xiv.

Books. (January 31, 1932), p.14.

New York Times Book Review. (February 7, 1932), p.12.

Outlook. Vol.160 (February 3, 1932), p.154.

Springfield Republican. (February 28, 1932), p.7e.

Wisconsin Library Bulletin. Vol.28 (March, 1932), p.91.

H85. Song of Roland (Translation)
Tablet. Vol.210 (October 19, 1957), p.334.

H86. Strong Poison
Booklist. Vol.27 (January, 1931), p.210.

Bookman. Vol. 72 (November, 1930), p.xxii.

Books. (October 26, 1930), p.20.

Boston Transcript. (December 13, 1930), p.2.

Cresset. Vol.38 (November, 1974), p.21.

Saturday Review. Vol.150 (October 11, 1930),
p.453.

Saturday Review of Literature. Vol.7 (December
20, 1930), p.478.

The Spectator. Vol.145 (November 15, 1930),
p.741.

Times Literary Supplement. (October 16, 1930),
p.841.

H87. Strong Poison; and Have His Carcase

Booklist. Vol.33 (January, 1937), p.162.

Chicago Daily Tribune. (September 12, 1936),
p.14.

New York Times Book Review. (August 30,
1936), p.20.

Wisconsin Library Bulletin. Vol.32 (November,
1936), p.111.

H88. Third Omnibus of Crime

Booklist. Vol.31 (May, 1935), p.301.

Books. (March 3, 1935), p.14.

Chicago Daily Tribune. (March 16, 1935), p.14.

New York Times Book Review. (March 24, 1935),
p.18.

Saturday Review of Literature. Vol.11
(March 9, 1935), p.358.

H89. The Unpleasantness at the Bellona Club

Best Sellers. Vol.30 (March 1, 1971), p.531.

Booklist. Vol.25 (December, 1928), p.125.

Bookman. Vol.68 (October, 1928), p.233.

Books. ₍New York Herald Tribune₎ (October
21, 1938), p.20.

Boston Transcript. (December 15, 1928), p.8.

Nation and Atheneum. Vol.43 (July 28, 1928),
p.564.

Saturday Review. Vol.146 (September 8, 1928),
p.305.

Saturday Review of Literature. Vol.5 (October
27, 1928), p.301.

Times Literary Supplement. (August 16, 1928),
p.594.

H90. Unpopular Opinions

Blackfriars. Vol.28 (August, 1947), p.382.

Booklist. Vol.44 (November 1, 1947), p.87.

Christian Century. Vol.64 (December 31,
1947), p.1616.

Dominicana. Vol.32 (December, 1947), pp.291-292.

Kirkus Reviews. Vol.15 (September 15, 1947), p.530.

New York Herald Tribune Weekly Book Review.
(October 5, 1947), p.10.

New York Times Book Review. (November 30,
1947), p.20.

H91. Whose Body?

Boston Transcript. (June 6, 1923), p.4.

Cleveland (July, 1923), p.51.

International Book Review. (September, 1923),
p.76.

Nation. Vol.117 (September 5, 1923), p.247.

New York Times Book Review. (May 27, 1923),
p.24.

New York World. (May 20, 1923), p.6e.

Springfield Republican. (September 16,
1923), p.7a.

Times Literary Supplement. (October 25, 1923),
p.709.

H92. The Zeal of Thy House

Booklist. Vol.34 (October 15, 1937), p.68.

Books. (December 12, 1937), p.29.

Commonweal. Vol.26 (October 15, 1937), p.582.

Living Church. Vol.97 (December 4, 1937),
p.721.

London Mercury. Vol.36 (July, 1937), p.277.

New Statesman and Nation. Vol.14 (September 11, 1937), p.384.

Time. Vol.30 (October 25, 1937), p.80.

Times Literary Supplement. (July 3, 1937), p.493.

Section I

Only the major sources for gathering information
on Dorothy L. Sayers and her writings are cited in
this section. Most of these are American, which
leaves some obvious gaps. For example, many reviews
of the author's works have appeared in British
newspapers and other periodical literature that we
have no access to here. Any great omissions will be
picked up in later editions of this work.

I. Bibliographies

I1. British Museum. Dept. of Printed Books. General
       Catalogue of Printed Books. London:
       Trustees, 1931+   v.1+
       Includes citations to most of the early
    and little known works of Miss Sayers.
I2. British National Bibliography. London: Council
       of the British National Bibliography,
       British Museum, 1950+   v.1+
       Includes citations of many works by Miss

Sayers published since 1950.

I3. Fiction Catalog. 7th ed. New York: H.W. Wilson,
    1960.   650p.

    Lists her detective fiction works along
with cuttings from reviews.

I4. Hagen, Ordean A. Who Done It? A Guide to Detective,
    Mystery, and Suspense Fiction. New York:
    Bowker, 1969.   834p.

    Includes an alphabetical listing of Sayers'
works on page 336.

I5. Herman, Linda. Corpus Delicti of Mystery Fiction:
    A Guide to the Body of the Case. With Beth
    Stiel. Metuchen, N.J.: Scarecrow Press, 1974.
    180p.

    Includes a short biographical sketch of
Miss Sayers and a listing of her detective
fiction in chronological order.

I6. Modern Humanities Research Association. Annual
    Bibliography of English Language and
    Literature. Cambridge [Eng.]: Cambridge
    University Press, 1920+   v.1+

    Lists a number of works by and about Miss
Sayers.

I7. Myers, Robin. A Dictionary of Literature in the
English Language, from Chaucer to 1940.
Oxford; New York: Pergamon Press, 1970+
v.1+

In Volume 1, page 755, Myers gives a very
short biographical note followed by a chronological listing of works by Miss Sayers.

I8. The New Cambridge Bibliography of English
Literature. Edited by I.R. Willison.
Cambridge: At the University Press, 1972.
5v.

Includes a chronological listing of works
by Miss Sayers on pages 730-731, in Volume 4.

I9. Sandoe, James. "Contribution Toward a Bibliography
of Dorothy L. Sayers," Bulletin of Bibliography, Vol.18 (May-August, 1944), pp.78-81.

The most extensive source of bibliographical
information on Miss Sayers. One must be careful,
however, because there are a number of errors
which are inevitable in a work of this type.

I10. U.S. Library of Congress. A Catalog of Books
Represented by Library of Congress Printed
Cards, Issued to July 31, 1942. Ann Arbor,
Mich.: Edwards, 1942-46.   167v.

Library of Congress and National Union Catalog.

Author Lists, <u>1942-1962</u>: <u>A</u> <u>Master</u>
<u>Cumulation</u>. Detroit: Gale Research Co.,
1969.   152p.

The <u>National</u> <u>Union</u> <u>Catalog</u>, <u>1956</u> <u>through</u> <u>1967</u>.
Totowa, N.J.: Rowman and Littlefield,
1970.   125p.

The <u>National</u> <u>Union</u> <u>Catalog</u>, <u>1968-1972</u>. Ann
Arbor, Mich.: Edwards, 1973.   119v.

The above represents the major sources for
bibliographical information on the works of
Dorothy L. Sayers in the United States. Annual
cumulations have been issued since 1972.

II. <u>Biographies</u>

Il1. <u>The</u> <u>American</u> <u>People's</u> <u>Encyclopedia</u>. New York:
Grolier, 1969.   20v.

A brief biographical sketch is given on
page 361 of Volume 16.

Il2. Babington, Margaret. "Miss Dorothy Sayers,"
<u>Times</u> (January 9, 1958), p.14e.

A letter on Miss Babington's association
with Dorothy L. Sayers, and her feelings
concerning this association.

I13. Brittain, Vera. <u>Testament of Youth; An
        Autobiographical Study of the Years,
        1900-1925</u>. New York: Macmillan, 1933.
        Brittain tells of her association with
     Dorothy L. Sayers at Oxford on pages 106-107
     of this work.

I14. <u>Chambers's Biographical Dictionary</u>. Revised
        edition. Edited by J.O. Thorne. New York:
        St. Martin's Press, 1962.   1432p.
        Includes a biographical sketch on page 1136.

I15. <u>The Concise Oxford Dictionary of English
        Literature</u>. 2d ed. Oxford: at the Clarendon
        Press, 1970.
        Includes a brief biographical sketch on
     pages 512 and 513.

I16. Drachmann, Aage Gerhardt. <u>Dorothy L. Sayers som
        Dramatiker, Essayist og Aestetiker</u>.
        København, G.E.C. Gad, 1959.   63p.
        (Studier fra sprog-/og oldtisdsforskning,
        nr. 238)
        A study both biographical and critical of
     Miss Sayers and her writings.

I17. <u>Enciclopedia</u> <u>dello</u> <u>Spettacolo</u>. Roma: Casa Ed.
le Maschere, 1954-1962.   9v.
Volume 8, page 1547, includes a brief
sketch in Italian.

I18. Hitchman, Janet. <u>Such</u> <u>a</u> <u>Strange</u> <u>Lady</u>: An
<u>Introduction</u> <u>to</u> <u>Dorothy</u> <u>L</u>. <u>Sayers</u> <u>(1893-</u>
<u>1957)</u>. London: New English Library, 1975.
203p.; New York: Harper & Row, 1975.   177p.
(The U.S. edition has the sub-title: <u>A</u>
<u>Biography</u> <u>of</u> <u>Dorothy</u> <u>L</u>. <u>Sayers</u>)
The first biographic attempt to discover
the woman who created the now world-famous
amateur sleuth, Lord Peter Wimsey. It reveals
the complex and diverse character of this
author-scholar who wrote in the wide spectrum
from detective fiction to theology.

I19. Kunitz, Stanley J., ed. <u>Twentieth</u> <u>Century</u> <u>Authors</u>...
With Howard Haycraft. New York: H.W. Wilson,
1942.   1577p.
-----. -----. <u>First</u> <u>Supplement</u>. Asst. ed. Vineta
Colby. New York: H.W. Wilson, 1955.   1123p.
Gives a relatively good biographical account
of Miss Sayers and her literary career up to

1955. See pages 1237-38 of the first volume
and page 874 of the Supplement.

I20. The New Century Handbook of English Literature.
Revised ed. Edited by Charles L. Barnhart
and W.D. Halsey. New York: Appleton-
Century-Crofts, 1967.
Includes a brief biographical sketch on
page 966.

I21. The Penguin Companion to Literature. I. Britain
and the Commonwealth. Edited by David Daiches.
Baltimore, Md.: Penguin Books, 1971.
Includes a good biographical sketch of
Miss Sayers, her life,and works on page 462.

I22. Smaridge, Norah. Famous British Women Novelists.
New York: Dodd, Mead, 1967.   127p.
Gives a biographical resume of Dorothy L.
Sayers' life and works on pages 100-108.

I23. Temple, Ruth, ed. Twentieth Century British
Literature: A Reference Guide and Bibliography.
With Martin Tucker. New York: F. Ungar,
1968.   261p.
Includes a biographical sketch on page 228.

I24. Wallace, Doreen. "Miss Dorothy L. Sayers,"
     Times (January 1, 1958), p.13b.

     A letter from Miss Wallace expressing her
feelings about Miss Sayers as a friend and
close associate.

I25. _Webster's Biographical Dictionary_. Springfield,
     Mass.: G. & C. Merriam Co., 1962.   1697p.

     Contains a very short biographical sketch
on page 1318.

III. _Indexes_

I26. Cook, Dorothy E. _The Short Story Index_. Edited
     with Isabel S. Munro. New York: H.W.
     Wilson, 1953.

     -----.-----. _Supplements_. 1954+   v.1+

     Lists a substantial number of Miss Sayers'
short stories and where they can be located.

I27. _Dramatic Criticism Index: A Bibliography of_
     Commentaries on Playwrights from Ibsen to
     the Avant-garde. Compiled and edited by
     Paul F. Breed and Florence M. Sniderman.
     Detroit, Mich.: Gale Research Co., 1972.
     1022p.

Lists several items on page 596.

I28. Essay and General Literature Index. New
York: H.W. Wilson, 1934+   v.1+
Lists a number of Sayers' essays and where
they can be located.

I29. Granger's Index to Poetry. 5th ed. Edited by
William F. Bernhardt. New York: Columbia
University Press, 1962.   2127p.
Lists a number of Miss Sayers' poems.

I30. International Index. New York: H.W. Wilson,
1916-1965+   v.1+
From 1965 to 1974: known as the Social
Sciences and Humanities Index; is now published
separately as the Social Sciences Index and the
Humanities Index. Includes articles, poetry, and
reviews appearing in the more specialized
periodical literature.

I31. Play Index. New York: H.W. Wilson, 1949+   v.1+
Includes a number of plays and broadcasts
by Miss Sayers. Also an adaptation.

I32. Readers' Guide to Periodical Literature. New
York: H.W. Wilson, 1905+   v.1+
Lists a number of Sayers' articles, short
stories, etc., along with reviews appearing in
the more general literature.

I33. Samples, Gordon. The Drama Scholars' Index to
Plays and Filmscripts: A Guide to Plays
and Filmscripts in Selected Anthologies,
Series and Periodicals. Metuchen, N.J.:
Scarecrow Press, 1974.

Lists The Zeal of Thy House on page 339.

IV. Obituaries

I34. Obituaries.

Americana Annual - 1958, p.542.

English. Vol.12 (Spring, 1958), p.10.

Illustrated London News. Vol.231 (December
28, 1957), p.1137. port.

New York Times. (December 19, 1957), p.29. port.

Newsweek. Vol.50 (December 30, 1957), p.45.

Publishers Weekly. Vol.173 (February 3,
1958), p.52.

Time. Vol. 70 (December 30, 1957), p.64.

Times. (December 19, 1957), p.12.

Wilson Library Bulletin. Vol.32 (February,
1958), p.392.

V. Portraits

135. Portraits.

    Bookman. ₍London₎ Vol.84 (April, 1933),
p.28a.

    Discovery.₍n.s.₎ Vol.1 (April, 1938), p.28.

    Illustrated London News. Vol.220 (February
2, 1952), p.184.

    Saturday Review of Literature. Vol.10
(July 7, 1934), p.795; Vol.12 (August 3, 1935),
p.4; Vol.13 (February 22, 1936), p.1; Vol.32
(July 16, 1949), p.15.

    Time. Vol.27 (February 24, 1936), p.75;
Vol.31 (February 28, 1938), p.67.

VI. Reviews

136. The Book Review Digest. New York: H.W. Wilson,
       1905+   v.1+

    Lists reviews from major periodicals.
Frequently includes brief excerpts from reviews.

137. Book Review Index. Detroit, Mich.: Gale Research
       Co., 1965+   v.1+

    Cites only reviews but is more extensive than

the <u>Book</u> <u>Review</u> <u>Digest</u> in that it covers a
greater number of periodicals.

Section J

<u>ADAPTATIONS</u>

In compiling this list of adaptations, I am
indebted to Jacqueline Kavanagh and the staff of
the B.B.C. Written Archives Centre; to Richard
Beynon and Ian Carmichael for their information
regarding the Lord Peter Wimsey television series;
and to William Everson for allowing me the use of his
lecture notes on <u>The Silent Passenger</u>.

This section is divided into five parts, each
centering on the type of work upon which the
adaptations are based: novels, short stories, religious
drama, translations, and even an unpublished story. (M.B.)

I. <u>Novels</u>

J1. <u>Busman's Honeymoon</u>. MGM-British Studios Ltd.,
    1940. (US: <u>Haunted Honeymoon</u>)
    Producer: Harold Huth
    Director: Arthur Woods
    Lord Peter: Robert Montgomery
    Harriet: Constance Cummings

Bunter: Sir Seymour Hicks

Insp. Kirk: Leslie Banks

Screenplay by Monckton Hoffe, Angus MacPhail,
    and Harold Goldman. Based upon the play
    by Dorothy L. Sayers and Muriel St.
    Clare Byrne.

According to Miss Byrne, neither she nor
Miss Sayers would have anything to do with
this film; and when it was released, they never
bothered to go see it. As it turns out, they
didn't miss much. Bosley Crowther gave it a
scathing review in the New York Times (October
31, 1940), 28:2. William Everson is a little
kinder, describing it as a "most enjoyable
light thriller" (The Detective in Film, Citadel
Press, 1972, p.193). For additional reviews
and photos, see:

Eames, John Douglas. The MGM Story. N.Y.:
Crown, 1975, p.165: a brief review, with a
photo of Montgomery, Cummings, Hicks, and Banks.

Everson, William K. The Detective in Film.
N.J.: Citadel Press, 1972, p.180: photo of
Montgomery and Robert Newton (as Frank Crutchley).

Gifford, Denis. The British Film Catalogue,
1895-1970. NY.: McGraw-Hill, 1973, 10724.

Illustrated London News. Vol.196 (August
31, 1940), p.292: photo of Montgomery, Cummings,
and Hicks.

New Statesman and Nation. Vol.20 (September
14, 1940), p.259.

Theatre Arts. Vol.24 (November, 1940),
p.787: photos.

Time. Vol.36 (November 18, 1940), p.85.

J2. Busman's Honeymoon. B.B.C. (Television),
    October 2, 1947.

Harold Warrender, Ruth Lodge, Ronald Adam,
Patric Curwen, Joan Hickson, Lewis Stringer,
Nellie Bowman, Sidney Tafler, Fred Essex, David
Garth, Brown Derby, and Kevin Sheldon.

J3. Busman's Honeymoon. B.B.C., Curtain Up!,
    August 3, 1949.

Stanley Groome, Ernest Sefton, Rita Vale,
Hugh Latimer, Susan Richmond, Geoffrey Lewis,
Charles Mortimer, David Kossoff, Dorothy Summers,
Eric Lugg, John Crocker, and Donald Gray.

J4. Busman's Honeymoon. B.B.C. (Television),
    October 3, 1957.

Peter Gray, Sarah Lawson, Charles Lloyd
Pack, George Woodbridge, Allan Jeayes, Ann
Pichon, Robert Hunter, Rita Webb, Arthur
Coullet, Warren Mitchell, Jeremy Longhurst,
Frank Pemberton, and Clive Batchelor.

J5. Busman's Honeymoon. B.B.C., Saturday Night
   Theatre, Repertory in Britain, June 19,
   1965.

Dorothy Reynolds, Angus Mackay, David
Monico, Michael Waddon-Pearce, Marion Forster,
Helen Dorward, David Belcher, Frank Woodfield,
Brian Petchey, Stanley Dawson, David Gilmore,
Michael Mollan, Roger Dyason, Producer: Anthony
Cornish.

J6. Clouds of Witness. B.B.C. (Television), April, 1972.
   Producer: Richard Beynon
   Director: Hugh David
   Lord Peter: Ian Carmichael
   Adapted by Anthony Steven

This, the first in the televised series of
the Lord Peter Wimsey novels, was very well-
received on both sides of the Atlantic (broadcast
in the U.S. by the Public Broadcasting Service
as part of its series, "Masterpiece Theatre,"
with introductory comments by Alistair Cooke).

Ian Carmichael's Wimsey is considerably
closer to Miss Sayers' masculine ideal
than either Robert Montgomery's or Peter
Haddon's in the earlier films (<u>Busman's
Honeymoon</u> and <u>The Silent Passenger</u>). The
entire series, in fact, is first-rate. For
reviews see:

The <u>Listener.</u> Vol.87 (April 13, 1972),
p.497.

New <u>York Times.</u> (October 17, 1973), 94:3;
and (December 2, 1973), II, 19:1, "Lord Peter
Wimsey Needs his Harriet," by Tabitha Powledge.

<u>Saturday Review World</u>. Vol.1 (October 9,
1973), p.38, "Will You Take Breakfast in Bed,
My Lord?"

<u>Times</u>.(April 6, 1972), p.10c.

J7. <u>Five Red Herrings</u>. B.B.C. (Television), March,
1975.

Producer: Bill Sellars

Director: Robert Tronson

Lord Peter: Ian Carmichael

Adapted by Anthony Steven

This was the fifth story adapted for the
Lord Peter Wimsey series, and, as of this

writing, it is to be the last program.
It appears that the B.B.C. had originally
planned to do nearly all of the novels (with
the exception, I think, of Whose Body?,
Unnatural Death, and perhaps Have His Carcase).
Strong Poison has been scripted, but there are
no plans for production since the B.B.C.
decided to cancel the series before Harriet
had a chance to show her face.

J8. Murder Must Advertise. B.B.C., A Book at Bedtime,
    November 21 - December 9, 1949.
    Read by Alan Wheatley.

J9. Murder Must Advertise. B.B.C., April 22, 1957.
    Ronald Barton, Malcolm Graeme, Juliet
    Callaway, Lockwood West, Malcolm Hayes, David
    Spenser, Eric Anderson, Joan Hart, Mollie Maureen,
    Elsa Palmer, Joan Sanderson, Nicky Elmett,
    Lewis Stringer, Beryl Calder, Virginia Winter,
    Trevor Martin, Shaun O'Riordan, Molly Rankin,
    Ronald Sidney, Hadyn Jones, and Will Leighton.

J10. Murder Must Advertise. B.B.C. (Television),
     June 1973.
     Producer: Richard Beynon

Director: Rodney Bennett

Lord Peter: Ian Carmichael

Adapted by Bill Craig

J11. The Nine Tailors. B.B.C., August 24, 1954 –
September 14, 1954. 4 episodes.

Marjorie Westbury, Alan Wheatley, Charles
Leno, James Thomason, Sylvia Coleridge, Janet
Morrison, Cyril Shaps, Allan Jeayes, Arthur
Ridley, Bryan Powley, Peter Claughton, Ernest
Jay, Ian Sadler, Sarah Leigh, Geoffrey Matthews,
Lewis Stringer, George Merritt, Manning Wilson,
Stephen Jack, Mairhi Russell, Geoffrey Wincott,
Ursula Hirst, Daphne Maddox, Frank Tickle, and
Mary Wimbush.

Recorded repeats of the series, April –
September, 1957.

J12. The Nine Tailors. B.B.C. (Television), April 1974.

Producer: Richard Beynon

Director: Raymond Menmuir

Lord Peter: Ian Carmichael

Adapted by Anthony Steven

J13. Strong Poison. B.B.C., Saturday Night Theatre,
Murder for Pleasure No.6, May 25, 1963.

Producer: Audrey Cameron

Peter Pratt, Frank Duncan, Lee Fox, Michael
Spice, Janet Burnell, Timothy West, James
Thomason, Norman, Vlaridge, Mary O'Farrell,
Mary Wimbush, Frank Partington, Margaret
Wolfit, Eric Anderson, Jo Manning Wilson,
Sheila Grant, Margot Boyd.

J14. The Unpleasantness at the Bellona Club. B.B.C.
(Television), January 1973.
Producer: Richard Beynon
Director: Ronald Wilson
Lord Peter: Ian Carmichael
Adaptor: Anonymous

J15. Whose Body? B.B.C., Mystery Playhouse, December 2,
1947 - January 6, 1948. 6 episodes.
Hugh Burden, Mary Clayton, Lionel Stevens,
Carl Bernard, Susan Richards, Vanessa Thornton,
Gladys Spencer, Ivan Samson, Deryck Guyler,
MacDonald Parke, Noel Dryden, Betty Linton,
Stanley Groome, Basil Jones, Harry Hutchinson,
Andrew Churchman, Malcolm Hayes, Donald Gray,
Arthur Ridley, Bryan Powley, Preston Lockwood,
Peter Creswell, Esme Lewis, Howard Marion
Crawford, Frances Clare, David Kossoff, et al.

II. Short Stories

J16. Absolutely Elsewhere. B.B.C., March 5, 1940.
   Announced in The Listener, (February 29,
   1940), p.444.

J17. Dilemma. B.B.C., Short Story: I., April 6,
   1934.

J18. In the Teeth of the Evidence. B.B.C., 1940. (?)
   This may have never been broadcast, although
   a contract was signed at the time.

J19. The Inspiration of Mr. Budd. B.B.C., August 10,
   1944.
   Arranged and produced by Marjorie Banks.
   Repeated, August 16, 1944.

J20. The Learned Adventure of the Dragon's Head. B.B.C.,
   Detectives in Fiction: III., June 10, 1938.
   Michael Shepley, Brembo Willia, Clive Baxter,
   Tom Macaulay, Cecil Trouncer, Arthur Owen, and
   H.O. Nicholson.

J21. The Learned Adventure of the Dragon's Head. B.B.C.,
   July 30, 1938.
   Robert Holland, Jack Melford, Philip Wade, Ivan
   Samson, Leslie Perrins, and Harcourt Williams.

J22. The Man Who Knew How. B.B.C., April 16, 1943.

      W.A. Tate, Lya Cavalcanti, M.A. Braune,

F.C. Hallawell, and E.C. Glass.

      Repeated, with the same contributors,

April 21, 1943.

J23. The Man Who Knew How. B.B.C., Appointment with

      Fear: V., April 23, 1946.

        Storyteller: Valentine Dyall

        Miss Pender: Marian Spencer

        Mr. Smith: Ivan Samson

        Charles Maunsell, Frank Atkinson, Preston

Lockwood, Charles Leno, Frank Partington.

J24. The Man With No Face. B.B.C., Saturday Night

      Theatre: I., April 3, 1943.

        Lord Peter: Robert Holmes

        Insp. Winterbottom: Antony Holles

        Salcombe Hardy: John Bryning

        Thomas Crowder: Ivor Barnard

        Grizelda Hervey, Ernest Sefton, Laidman

Browne, Bryan Powley, Sybil Arundale, Preston

Lockwood, Belle Chrystall.

J25. The Man With the Copper Fingers. B.B.C., Story

      of Crime and Detection, November 12, 1968.

J26. <u>Seeds</u> <u>of</u> <u>Suspicion</u>. John McGreevey. Chicago:
Dramatic Publishing Co., 1951.   24p.
One act. 4 men. 4 women. 1 interior.
Based upon the short story "Suspicion," in
which a housekeeper is suspected of being an
arsenical poisoner. (Source: <u>Play</u> <u>Index</u>,
1949-52. N.Y.: H.W. Wilson, 1953)

J27. <u>Striding</u> <u>Folly</u>. B.B.C., 1943. (?)
This may have never been broadcast, although
a contract was signed at the time.

J28. <u>Suspicion</u>. B.B.C., 1943. (?)
This may have never been broadcast, although
a contract was signed at the time.

III. <u>Religious</u> <u>Drama</u>

J29. <u>He</u> <u>That</u> <u>Should</u> <u>Come</u>, <u>A</u> <u>Nativity</u> <u>Play</u>. B.B.C.
(Television), December 24, 1948.
Originally written for radio (see D12).
Oliver Burt, Geoffrey Dunn, Glyn Lawson,
Laurice Bannister, Christopher Gill, Willoughby
Gray, Hugh Moxey, Stanley Lemin, Elizabeth Maude,
Joseph O'Connor, Joanna Horder, Alan Wheatley,
Andrew Leigh, Leonard White, Frank Coburn, John
Vere, Evelyn Moore, Peter George, Kenneth Cleveland,
and Anna Somerset.

J30. The Just Vengeance. B.B.C., March 30, 1947.

      Originally, the Lichfield Festival play
for 1946 (see D6).

      Valentine Dyall, Lewis Stringer, Catherine
Salkeld, Mary Kenton, Neville Mapp, Leonard
Sachs, Deryk Guyler, Robert Farquharson, John
Garside, Francis de Wolff, Sebastion Cabot,
Madeleine Burgess, Lorna Davis, Edith
Savile, William Forbes, Seymour Green, Monica
Stracey, Charles Rennison, Alwyne Whatsley,
Gabrielle Blunt, Cyril Gardiner, Raf de la Torre,
Lionel Stevens, Malcolm Hayes, Heron Carvic,
Molly Rankin, Susan Richards, Andrew Churchman,
David Stringer, Frank Atkinson, and Vanessa
Thornton.

IV. Translations

J31. The Song of Roland. Translated from the French
      by Dorothy L. Sayers. Read by Anthony Quayle.
      Edited for Caedmon Records by Barbara
      Holdridge. N.Y.: Caedmon Records Inc.,
      [196-?]   #TC 2059.
      LP 33 1/3 rpm   stereo   4 sides

On back cover: an excerpt from the
Introduction to her translation of <u>The</u> <u>Song</u>
<u>of</u> <u>Roland</u>, Penguin Classics, 1957.

V. <u>Original</u> <u>Story</u> <u>(Unpublished)</u>

J32. <u>The</u> <u>Silent</u> <u>Passenger</u>.   Phoenix Films, 1935.
        Producer: Hugh Perceval
        Director: Reginald Denham
        Editor: Thorold Dickinson
        John Ryder: John Loder
        Lord Peter: Peter Haddon
        Mollie Ryder: Mary Newland
        Parker: Austin Trevor
        Bunter: Aubrey Mather
        Donald Wolfit, Leslie Perrins, Ralph Truman,
            Gordon McLeod, George de Warfaz, Vincent
            Holman, Ann Codrington, Dorice Fordred,
            and Annie Esmond.
        Screenplay by Basil Mason, based upon an
            original story by Dorothy L. Sayers.
    A high-class "B" movie with lots of surprises
and a good mystery, based upon a story written
<u>solely</u> for the purpose of this film venture. In

a letter dated January 19, 1976, Charles Shibuk
indicates that "it was _not_ written for any
kind of publication, nor based on a previously
published story.... This film showed "who done
it" well before Lord Peter appeared on the screen."

Peter Haddon's Wimsey is less than the
masculine ideal, a bit too silly-ass (even
for Peter Wimsey), and played largley for
comedy. John Ryder, the real hero of the film,
sets out to capture the killer of his wife's
blackmailer in a highly suspenseful chase sequence
shot on location in a London railway yard, and
highlighted by an unforgettable visual shock.
One of the most descriptive accounts of the film
can be found in William Everson's The Detective
in Film (Citadel Press, 1972, pp.192-193). For
a review see New Statesman and Nation, Vol.10
(July 20, 1935), p.95. See also Denis Gifford's
British Film Catalogue (McGraw-Hill, 1973,
09794).

A CHRONOLOGY

In order to place the works of Dorothy L. Sayers in historical perspective, the following chronological list is provided. Although not all single items are listed, this progression should reveal a general pattern in her writings--from poetry to detective fiction, to religious writings, to Dante.

1916: Op. I. (A collection of poetry)

1918: Catholic Tales and Christian Songs (A collection of poetry)

1923: Whose Body? (A detective novel)

1926: Clouds of Witness (A detective novel)

1927: Unnatural Death (U.S. title: The Dawson Pedigree) (A detective novel)

1928: Great Short Stories... (An edited collection of short stories)

Lord Peter Views the Body (A collection of short stories)

The Unpleasantness at the Bellona Club (A detective novel)

1929: The Omnibus of Crime (An edited collection
of short stories)

Tristan in Brittany (A translation)

1930: The Documents in the Case (A detective novel
written in collaboration with Robert Eustace)

Strong Poison (A detective novel)

1931: Five Red Herrings (U.S. title: Suspicious
Characters) (A detective novel)

The Floating Admiral (A detective novel written
in collaboration with others)

Great Short Stories..., 2d Series (An edited
collection of short stories)

1932: Have His Carcase (A detective novel)

Second Omnibus of Crime (An edited collection
of short stories)

1933: Ask a Policeman (A detective novel written in
collaboration with others)

Hangman's Holiday (A collection of short stories)

Murder Must Advertise (A detective novel)

1934: Great Short Stories..., 3d Series (An edited
collection of short stories)

The Nine Tailors (A detective novel)

1935: Gaudy Night (A detective novel)

Third Omnibus of Crime (An edited collection of
short stories)

1936: <u>Busman's Honeymoon</u> (A play)

He <u>That Should Come</u> (A radio play)

<u>Tales of Detection</u> (An edited collection of
short stories)

1937: <u>Busman's Honeymoon</u> (The detective novel version
of the play)

<u>Zeal of Thy House</u> (A play)

1939: <u>Devil to Pay</u> (A play)

<u>Double Death</u> (A detective novel written in
collaboration with others)

In <u>the Teeth of the Evidence</u> (A collection of
short stories)

<u>Strong Meat</u> (A religious tract)

1940: <u>Begin Here</u>... (Book-length essay)

<u>Love All</u> (A play)

1941: <u>Golden Cockerel</u> (A radio play)

<u>The Man Born to Be King</u> (A radio play cycle)

<u>The Mind of the Maker</u> (Book-length essay)

1944: <u>Even the Parrot</u> (A children's book)

1946: <u>The Just Vengeance</u> (A play)

<u>Unpopular Opinions</u> (A collection of essays)

Dante. <u>The Heart of Stone</u> (A translation)

1947: <u>Creed or Chaos</u>? (A collection of essays)

<u>The Lost Tools of Learning</u> (A pamphlet)

1949: Dante. The Divine Comedy: Cantica I, Hell
      (A translation)

1951: The Emperor Constantine (A play)

1952: Christ's Emperor (A play)

1953: The Days of Christ's Coming (A children's booklet)

      The Story of Adam and Christ (A pamphlet)

1954: Introductory Papers on Dante (A collection of essays)

1955: Dante. The Divine Comedy: Cantica II, Purgatory
      (A translation)

1956: The Story of Noah's Ark (A pamphlet)

1957: Further Papers on Dante (A collection of essays)
      The Song of Roland (A translation)

1962: Dante. The Divine Comedy: Cantica III, Paradise
      (A translation completed by Barbara Reynolds)

1963: The Poetry of Search and the Poetry of Statement
      (A posthumously published collection of essays)

THE DOROTHY L. SAYERS PAPERS

Through the courtesy of Barbara J. Griffin
of the Marion E. Wade Collection at Wheaton College,
we are including the following checklist of Miss
Sayers' papers. All of these manuscripts are open
to the public.

The Wrecker
  film scenario
  ms. 21 pp.
  about train wrecking or sabotage

The Zeal of Thy House
  play
  ms. 150 full pp. 10 piece pp.
  photographs 2
  typed pp. 49

The Image in the Mirror
  detective story
  ms. 45 pp.

The Queen's Square
  detective story
  ms. 24 pp.

The Man Who Knew How
  detective story
  ms. 25 pp.

The Fountain
  detective story
  ms. 21 pp.
  2/3 of page seven missing

Absolutely Elsewhere
    detective story
    ms. 26 pp.

Dilemma
    detective story
    ms. 25 pp.

An Arrow O'er the House
    detective story
    ms. 20 pp.

Scrawns
    detective story
    ms. 21 pp.

Nebuchadnezzar
    short story
    ms. 16 pp.
    biblical _themes_, at least

Blood-Sacrifice
    detective story
    ms. 45 pp.
    about John Scales, Old Florrie and theatre

Suspicion
    detective story
    ms. 29 pp.

The Cyprian Cat
    detective story
    ms. 20 pp.

Cat's Cradle, A Comedy in Three Acts
    detective story
    ms. 20 pp.

Unfinished story, Introducing Lord Peter
    ms. 47 pp.

The Master Key - a Lord Peter Wimsey Story
    short story, unfinished
    ms. 15 pp.

Spick and Span
      detective story, unfinished
      ms. 10 pp.

The Situations of Judkin
      short story
      ms. 35 pp.
      1. The Traveling Rug

Herod the Great
      play
      ms. Act I, 24 pp. (first set)
           Act I, 26 pp. typed pp. 8
           Act I, typed pp. 23 (third set)
      ms. 34 pp.
      typed pp. 2

                  "The Scoop"

T.S.S. of Broadcast and Novel Versions (incomplete)
Notes and Summaries etc.
M.S.S. of D.L.S. chapter and notes

27 pp. manuscript - chapter 12, "The Final Scoop" (Sayers)
Synopsis for Radio Times - 4 pages typed
Carbon typed pages - 15 (7 of these are duplicates)
"   "   "   - 7 (purple carbon)

More typed pages - 8
Typed and carbon pages - 28
All the above is synopsis and notes, horribly jumbled
      and confusing
Broadcast Version - 3 typed pages
Broadcast Version - apparently complete, 18 typed pages
      pages - "Over the Wire," by Dorothy L. Sayers.
Carbon of chapter 3 (E.C. Bentley), "Fisher's Alibi" -
      9 pages
Carbon of chapter 5 (Anthony Berkeley), "Tracing Tracy" -
      9 pages
Carbon of part VI   (Freeman Wills Crofts), "Scotland
      Yard on the Job" - 13 pages
Another carbon of part VI - 10 pages
Carbon of chapter 7 (Clemence Dane), "Beryl in Broad
      Street"

Carbon of chapter 10 (Miss Clemence Dane), "Beryl
    Takes the Consequences" - 8 pages
Another carbon of chapter 10 - 8 pages
Carbon of chapter 11 (F.W. Crofts) - 11 pages
Another carbon of chapter 11 - 13 pages
Carbon of The Scoop (expanded version), chapter 1 by
    D.L. Sayers - 20 pages
Corrected carbon of above version, here called
    "Broadcast Version" - 20 pages
Carbon of Part II, by Agatha Christie - 24 pages
Typescript of Part III, I suppose (it is untitled);
    I don't know who wrote it - 15 pages
Typescript of Part IV, (no author's name given), "The
    Weapon" - 17 pages
Typescript of novel version of chapter 6 (F.W. Crofts) -
    25 pages
Carbon of the above - 25 pages
Carbon of chapter 9 (Anthony Berkeley) - 14 pages
Typescript of novel version of chapter 11 (Crofts) -
    27 pages
Carbon of the above - 27 pages
Typescript of chapter 12 (D.L. Sayers), with hand-
    written note by her on page 1, 14 pages plus
    five copies of the map of "The Scoop" story

                    Unpopular Opinions

Ms. of "Towards a Christian Aesthetic" - 14 pp.
Ms. of "Creative Mind" - 20 pp.
Ms. of "The Gulf Stream and the Channel" - 11 pp.
Ms. of "They Tried to be Good" - 6 pp. front and back
Ms. of "Dr. Watson, Widower" - 26 pp.
Ms. of unidentified story told in first person -
    7 pp. front and back
Galley proofs, in part corrected by author (Dr. Kilby's
    note)

Untitled essay or address on the subject of murder
    ms. 15 pp.
    apparently satirical

Untitled essay or address on the nature of machines and
    man
    ms. 7 pp.

The Modern Detective Story
        address to the Sesame Imperial Club, 27/10/36
        ms. 8 pp.

Detectives in Fiction
        essay or address
        ms. 6 pp.

"Arsenic Probably" (Topical: Mr. Gay's Goldfish)
        ms. 3 pp.
        rejection slip from The Daily News attached)
        on arsenic poisoning of course

Untitled address on the craft of detective fiction
        ms. 6 pp.
        typescript of same, corrected 12 pp.
        ms. 3 additional pp.

In England - Now
"Rambling Meditations on the Subject of 'Christian Duty'"
        ms. 22 pp.
        galley proofs .
        ms. 14 pp.

Untitled story about a girl named Griselda and the
        theft of a jewel from a church
        ms. 7 pp.

Craft of Detective Fiction
        address outline
        ms. 14 pp.

Address to the Detection Club
        ms. 6 pp.

Origines du Roman Policier
        speech delivered in French
        ms. 12 pp.

The Comedy of Horrors
        essay or address
        ms. 12 pp.

Trent's Last Case
        book review?
        ms. 5 pp.

I You Want War _____
    essay or address
    ms. 4 pp.
    on peacemongers

The Importance of Being Vulgar
    untitled speech
    ms. 23 pp.

The Just Vengeance - The Lichfield Festival Play for
    1946
    ms. 82 pp.

He That Should Come - a Nativity Play for Broadcasting
    ms. 25 pp.
    also a copy of the music for "He That Should
    Come," 24 sheets

Gaudy Night
    ms. 639 pp.

The Five Red Herrings
    ms. 509 pp.
    has the first title as "The Six Suspects"

Unnatural Death
    ms. 333 pp.
    one page missing at the end of the second block;
    last two chapters missing

Strong Poison
    ms. 369 pp.

Have His Carcase
    ms. 230 pp.
    notes 8 pp.
    letters giving information she used in this novel,
    45 pp.

Talboys
    typed pp. 36

Smith and Smith - Removals (both parts)
    detective story, not Lord Peter
    ms. 59 pp.

The Haunted Policeman
     short story
     ms. 33 pp.
     carbon typescript - 31 pp.

        The Man Born to be King

(play; manuscript unless otherwise indicated)
Introduction - 33 pp.
Kings in Judea - 7 pp.
First Play - Scene 2 (Bethlehem), Sequence 1 - 14 pp.
First Play - Scene 2, Sequence 2 - 6 pp.
First Play - Scene 3 - 14 pp.
Second Play - Scene 1 - two versions - 42 pp.
Second Play - Scene 2 - 19 pp.
Third Play - Scene 1 - 25 pp.
Third Play - Scene 2 - 19 pp.
Fourth Play - 42 pp.
Fifth Play - 48 pp.
Fifth Play - Scene 5 - 7 pp.
Sixth Play - 48 pp.
Seventh Play - 53 pp.   typed pp. 12
Eighth Play - 57 pp.
Ninth Play - 57 pp.
Tenth Play - 42 pp.
Eleventh Play - 43 pp.   typed pp. 4
Twelfth Play - 47 pp.

"Murder Must Advertise - The Original Manuscript"
     ms. 460 pp.
     chapters 1-21 (last three pages advertising and
     possible titles)
     in black box, loose pages
     some corrections, probably not exactly as published

Printed maps of town: Fenchurch St. Paul (Nine Tailors)

   "Ask a Policeman Detection Club Material"
          (folder)

I. The Conclusions of Mr. Roger Sheringham
     recorded by D.L. Sayers.
     ms. 62 pp.
     (Boonin in Wade Collection of which this is one
     chapter??)

II. Ask a Policeman, Part I
    by John Rhode
    carbon of a typescript   71 pp.

III. Ask a Policeman (Synopsis of Part I)
    typed pp. 11

Christmas Card Texts

(The Days of Christ's Coming) - The Christmas Story
        ms.   6 pp.
        (published by Hamish Hamilton)

(The Story of the Easter) - Betrayal, Death and
        Ressurection
        ms.   9 pp.

(Noah's Ark)
        ms.   3 pp.
        typed pp. 3 (same as manuscript)

The Tale of Adam and Eve
        poetry: 27 poems from "Adam and Eve," to "The
        Last Judgement"
        ms. 14 pp.
        ms.   5 pp. "Suggestions for the artist" and cover
        texts

The Enchanted Garden
        ms. 10 pp.
        ms.   3 pp. "Descriptions" (for the artist)
        typed pp. +2 (same as above, 15 total typed?)

Notebook:

        notes for a P.W. book
        ms.   8 pp.

        quotations
        ms.   2 pp.

        The Romance of Tristan
        ms. 38 pp.
        going one way

        The Fascinating Problem of Uncle Meleager's Will
        ms. 37 pp.
        going other way

        The Horrible Story of the Missing Molar
        ms.   6 pp.

Stocking knitting directions
ms. 2 pp.

"It's very unpleasant to acknowledge oneself -
especially to a lady - to be a fool."
ms. 2 pp.
in pencil, personal letter?

Stitching **Folly**
    detective story
    ms. 20 pp.
    typed pp. 21

The Mind of the Maker

I. Preface, some corrections throughout - 6 pp.
I. The Laws of Nature and Opinion - 15 pp.
II. The Image of God - 10 pp.
III. The Trinity of Man the Maker - 11 pp.
IV. The Energy Revealed in Creation - 12 pp.
V. Freewill and Miracle - 22 pp.
VI. The Energy Incarnate in Self-Expression - 6 pp.
VII. Associated Passages
    Quotations from literature and the Bible on angels
    typed pp. 2
VII. Maker of All Things - 14 pp.
VIII. Pentecost - 16 pp.
IX. The Love of the Creature - 18 pp.
X. Scalene Trinities - 36 pp. (a few appear to be notes)
XI. Loose pages (hard to identify)
    Problem Picture - 23 pp.
    Single-spare A (Eddington quote and comment) - 1 p.
    "On these four characteristics of the detective
    problem" - 3 pp.
    typed pages:
    "224" - 1 p.
    "207-210" - $4\frac{1}{2}$ pp.
    "198-206" - $8\frac{1}{2}$ pp. ("Problem Picture" crossed out)
    "212 and 213" - 2 pp.
    "214-217" - 4 pp.
    "218-231" - 6 pp.
    13 miss. manuscript pages

Sequel to Busman's Honeymoon (incomplete)
    ms. 176 pp.

          Constantine: Christ's Emperor

I.   Constantine, Colchester 1951
        black notebook
        ms. 14 pp.
Saint Anne's Group Presents "Christ's Emperor,"
        being the second part of the Colchester Festival
        Play by D.L. Sayers...
        ms. 11 pp. of stage directions and biblical
        quotations
II.   The Emperor Constantine Cast
        blue notebook
        ms. 74 pp. (some printed)
        names, addresses, measurements, etc.
        probably not by D.L. Sayers
IV.   Introduction to the play's history - 9 pp.
V.   Act I - 63 pp.
VI.   Act II - 60 pp.
VII.   Act III - 100 pp. (some scenes missing)
VIII.   Epilogue - 6 pp.
IX.   Program note
        ms. 2 pp. introduction to the play
        ms. 7 pp. (a brief play of introduction?)
X.   notes on costume, cast and scenery
        ms. 18 pp. (most not D.L. Sayers' handwriting)
        typed inventory of scenery pieces left from
        previous plays
XI.   Anthony Fleming Esq., 1 Boltons, London, S.W. 10
        blue folder with A. Fleming's name on the cover
        Green notebook inside folder
            publisher's proof
            promptcopy for players
            notes (most not by D.L. Sayers)
        typed? 212 pp.

Printed illustration of "The Dragon's Head" for a
        short story in Lord Peter Views the Body

The Unsolved Puzzle of the Man with no Face
        ms. 33½ pp.
        note says: about 11 pp. missing at the end

The Piscatorial Farce of the Stolen Stomach
        ms. 33 pp.
        note says: short passage missing at end

The Undignified Melodrama of the Bone of Contention
        ms. 16 pp.
        followed by note: about 6 pp. missing
        ms. 1 pp.
        followed by note: about two pp. missing
        ms. 57 pp.
        followed by note: 3 pp. missing
        ms. 1 pp.
        followed by note: 3 pp. missing
        ms. 6 pp.
        drawn map to illustrate
        about half of the manuscript is illegible due
        to stains

                The Song of Roland

            (13 rules notebook pads)

Introductory material: The Feudal Picture
I.   ms. 41 pp.
        ms. 89 pp. of translation
            some pages with just four or five lines, most
            pages less than half full
Translation:
        II.   ms. 15 pp.
        III.   ms. 33 pp.
        IV.   ms. 23 pp.
        V.   ms. 5 pp.
        VI.   ms. 41 pp.
        VII.   ms. 6 pp.
        VIII.   ms. 18 pp.
        IX.   ms. 30 pp.
        X.   ms. 21 pp.
        XI.   ms. 46 pp.
        XII.   ms. 19 pp.
        XIII.   ms. 11 pp. outline and notes for "Roland"
                ms. 1 p. evidently notes for a detective story
                ms. 1 p. note about "C.W. paper," and "Ch. W"
Roland
        ms. 28 pp.
        typed pp. 2
        evidently part of the text for the introduction

The Floating Admiral
      Shock for the Inspector
      chapter VII by D.L. Sayers
      ms. 52 pp.

The Story According to D.L.L. [D.L.S.?]
      ms. 28 pp.
      notes on chapter VII
      ms. 7 pp.

The Story According to D.L.S.
      typed pp. 12
      ms. 1 p. note
      ms. 26 pp. summarizing story
      ms. 13 pp. notes and queries

Behind the Screen

I.   Part 3 Synopsis Behind the Screen
       typed carbon 4 pp.
II.   Chapter VI, Mr. Parsons on the Case
       typed carbon with handwritten corrections 9 pp.
III.   Synopsis of Behind the Screen (Hugh Walpole)
       typed carbon 11 1/8 pp.
       "with compliments of the BBC"
IV.   Behind the Screen Chapter IV (Anthony Berkeley)
       typed carbon 3 pp.
V.   Chapter VI, Mr. Parsons on the Case
       typed carbon 8 pp.
VI.   Chapter IV, In the Aspidistin (Anthony Berkeley)
       typed carbon 13 pp.
VII.   Part I (E.C. Bentley)
       typed carbon 9 pp.
VIII. Chapter V (E.C. Bentley)
IX.   Chapter IV (Anthony Berkeley)
X.   timeschedule
       ms. 1 p.
XI.   Chapter III
       ms. 3 pp.
XII.   Chapter Headings
       ms. 2 pp.
XIII. "Quite. And you knew..."
       ms. 1 p.
XIV. Suggested Solutions
       ms. 6 pp.

XV.   Synopsis
        ms. 5 pp.
XVI.   Chapter III (D.L. Sayers)
        ms. 16 pp.
XVII.   Part III (D.L. Sayers)
        ms. 18 pp.

                Even the Parrot

I.   "rough proof only"
        frontpiece 18 pp. (+ illustrations)
        a few comments in D.L. Sayers' handwriting?
II.   "first proof" - 12 pp.
III.   ms. 22 pp. (most on verso)

... Who Calls the Tune
        short story
        ms. 10 pp.
        discussion between a devil and an angel about
        the value of a dead man's works

Talboys
        ms. 33 pp.

Speech given at Oxford; proposing the toast of the
        University of Oxford
        in exercise book, ms. 11 pp.
        "I am going to tell you quite seriously what I
        think of the University"

            Wilkie Collins and Peter Wimsey
                (exercise book)

I.   The Adventures of the Cat in the Bay
        ms. 33 pp.
II.   The Tooth of Time
        unfinished essay of the Even the Parrot type
        ms. 4 pp.
III.   N or M
        unfinished essay
        ms. 4 pp.
        about names of characters and titles of books
IV.   Wilkie Collins
        list of letters
        ms. 3 pp.

V.   Bibliography for study of Wilkie Collins (and
      Charles Dickens?)
      ms. 12 pp.

Busman's Honeymoon

I.   A Detective Comedy in Three Acts by D.L. Sayers
      and M. St. Clove Bylue [M. St. Clare Byrne]
      ms. 3 pp. author's note
      ms. 13 pp. (not all in D.L. Sayers' handwriting)
      typed pp. 2
      typed carbon 3 pp.
      ms. 25 pp. in D.L. Sayers' handwriting with
      corrections in another hand
II.   Busman's Honeymoon, A Murder Theme with Sentiment
      by D.L. Sayers
      ms. 382 pp.

The Documents in the Case

(in black box with "The Documents in the Case by Dorothy
L. Sayers and Robert Eustace" "The Original Manuscript"
written on it)

I.   Section I: Synthesis
      ms. 213 pp.
II.   Section II: Analysis
      ms. 176 pp.

The Nine Tailors

I.   Red Exercise Book titled "The Nine Tailors, notes
      and changes of Bell-ringing plot outline in part MS."
      ms. 5 pp. of names, inscriptions and descriptions
      ms. 13 pp. on change-ringing + number for bells
      ms. 24 pp.
      ms. 18 pp. plot outline and notes on change-ringing
II.   maps of the area of Fenchurch St. Paul
III.a ms. 24 pp. of maps, drawings, listing, etc., plus
      plot outline
III.b Chapter I - 32 pp.
         "   II - 37 pp.
         "   III - 32 pp.
         "   IV - 32 pp.

"   V - 32 pp.
"   VI - 28 pp.
"   VII - 26 pp.
"   VIII - 22 pp.
"   IX - 19 pp.
"   X - 26 pp.
"   XI - 17 pp.
"   XII - 20 pp.
"   XIII - 11 pp.
"   XIV - 18 pp.
"   XV - 13 pp.
"   XVI - 16 pp.
"   XVII - 16 pp.
"   XVIII - 12 pp.
"   XIX - 17 pp.
"   XX - 6 pp.

The Unpleasantness at the Bellona Club

I.   Green notebook
      ms. 46 pp.
      The Mousehole: A Detective Fantasia in Three Flats,
      Act I
      ms. 11 pp.
II.   Chapter IV
      ms. 28 pp.
      faded and stained
III. ms. 182 pp.
      faded and stained

INDEX

Ask a Policeman, A12
Atlantic Monthly, E56

Babington, Margaret. Miss Dorothy Sayers, I12
Baker, Albert Edward, ed. Christian Basis for the
    Post-War World, C109
Baker-Street Studies, H.W. Bell, C110
Barnhart, Charles L. - See I20
Barton, Dr. Eustace Robert, collaborator on the novel:
    The Documents in the Case, A13
Barzun, Jacques. A Catalogue of Crime, H15; Delights
    of Detection, B59
Basney, Lionel. God and Peter Wimsey, H1
Bauer, William F., ed. Short Stories in Parallel, B60
Beatrician Vision in Dante and Other Poets:
        Essay, C5
        Lecture, G3
Bedside Tales, B61
Beecroft, John - See B85
Begin Here: A War-Time Essay (also: A Statement of
        Faith):
        Book-length essay, C91
        Review, H51
Behind the Screen - III, D10
Bell, Howard Wilmerding, ed. Baker-Street Studies, C110
Bentley, Edmund C. Greedy Night, H16; Second Century of
    Detective Stories, B62
Berbrich, Joan D., comp. Stories of Crime and Detection,
    B63
Bergin, Thomas G. Dante, H17
Berkeley, Anthony - See B110
Bernhardt, William F. - See I29
Best Mystery Stories, M. Richardson, B106
Bibliographies, pp.219-222
Bibulous Business of a Matter of Taste, B5
Biographical Note (on Lord Peter Wimsey), C93
Biographical Sources, pp.222-226
Bitter Almonds, B6
Blood Sacrifice, B7
Bloodhound into Bridegroom, K. Simonds, H38
Bond, Raymond T. Famous Stories of Code and Cipher,
    B64; Handbook for Poisoners, B65
Book Review Digest, I36
Book Review Index, I37
Bowden, W. Paul - See B60
Boy's Second Book of Great Detective Stories, H. Haycraft,
    B83